Bridging the Gap: Addressing Heterogeneity in Local Models for Enhanced Multiparty Learning

Naviya

Contents

1 Introduction

1.1 Blockchain-Empowered Secure Machine Learning

In the big data era, one of the most critical intelligent applications is multiparty learning or federated learning[68]. In particular, as institutions, companies, and smart devices are collecting huge amounts of data every day, it is inefficient and insecure to collect and learn on all the data together at a single location. In contrast, in multiparty learning, the learning is conducted in a distributed fashion, where each party can keep their data local.

Most existing multiparty learning systems only focus on training a global model for all the parties, ignoring the fact that a local model may have already been trained at each party based on its own dataset. Effectively utilizing these local models can substantially improve the training efficiency of multiparty learning. For example, McMahan et al.[42] and Li et al.[34] use model averaging in multiparty learning, and further propose Byzantine attack resilient model averaging methods. However, these works assume that the local models at each party are homogeneous, which may not be practical. A few works try to address this issue. For instance, Wu et al.[69] propose a multiparty multiclass margin to calibrate heterogeneous local models

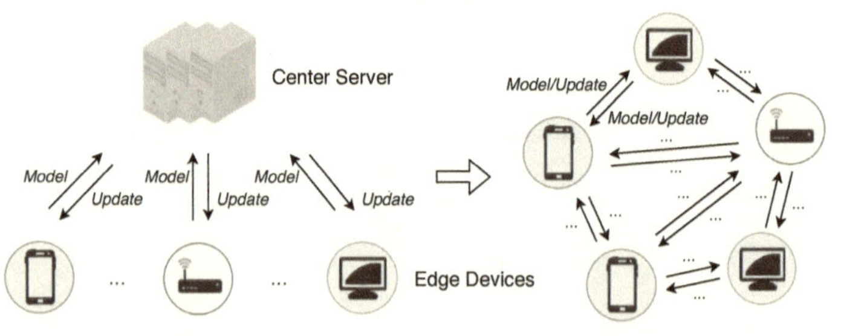

Figure 1.1. Different structures for distributed and decentralized multiparty learning.

in the system. Note that all these works rely on a trusted central server to coordinate the distributed learning process, which obviously becomes a single point of failure and can be subject to attacks. Only a couple of works like[31] attempt to design decentralized multiparty learning systems. Note that only linear models are considered in[31]. To the best of our knowledge, secure decentralized multiparty learning with heterogeneous models remains an open and challenging problem.

In this section, we propose a novel secure decentralized multiparty learning system by taking advantage of the blockchain technology, called BEMA. In particular, each party in a decentralized system broadcasts its local model, and meanwhile, processes the received (heard) models from other parties over his local dataset, and identifies the models that need to be calibrated. Following our designed protocol, the party sends the calibration message to the corresponding parties. In so doing, the parties in the system do not need to share their whole dataset with other parties. In this system, we consider two types of Byzantine attacks in the system, which can occur in model broadcasting and model calibration processes. To protect system security, we carefully design "off-chain sample mining" and "on-chain mining" schemes. Theoretical analysis is performed to show that the proposed system has bounded performance under Byzantine attacks. The main contributions of blockchain-empowered machine learning are summarized as follows:

- We propose a novel blockchain-empowered decentralized secure multiparty learning system called BEMA, where learning parties hold heterogeneous local models.

- We formulate two types of Byzantine attacks in the system, and devise secure "off-chain sample mining" and "on-chain mining" schemes to defend against the attacks.

- We theoretically analyze the performance of the proposed system and prove that it is bounded under Byzantine attacks.

- We evaluate the system with the real-world dataset. We show that the proposed system has a comparable performance compared with traditional multiparty learning with a central server, and is resilient to Byzantine attacks.

1.2 Blockchain-Empowered Application in Smart Transportation - TrafficChain

Intelligent Connected Vehicles (ICVs) aim to provide smart, safe, and efficient transportation services by exploiting multiple modern technologies, including communications, computing, data mining, deep learning. Intel has predicted that vehicles will produce 4,000 GB of data every day by 2025[25]. Properly utilizing and mining the data provided by smart vehicles, ICVs would be able to support various services such as dynamic routing[51], traffic incident detection[71], autonomous driving[57].

Introduction

Despite having been studied for years, the current transportation infrastructure and systems are still simple and quite traditional. Many problems are still open and extensive efforts are required to fulfill the mission of ICVs. In particular, real-time traffic status is crucial information for vehicles to plan their routes to avoid congestion or road incidents, like accidents and road closure, and can greatly save people's travel time. Currently, people usually use popular navigation agents like Apple map and Google map to help plan travel routes. A driver can send his/her current location and the destination to the service provider through smartphones or navigation devices to acquire navigation guide. By collecting and mining the real-time travel data from a large number of users' smartphones, the traffic map service providers like Apple and Google are able to provide the traffic status on the roads. However, such navigation agents raise several major concerns. First, current navigation systems are centralized and vulnerable to congestion and a single point of failure. Second, current navigation systems like Apple map or Google map collect real-time information from users and has already compromised users' privacy. For example, they can know users' home and work addresses and hence their identities, track them in real-time, etc. Third, users have no control over the security of current navigation systems. If compromised, the navigation systems can not only deliberately return malicious route plans to users, but also track users and cause serious security concerns.

The emergence of blockchain provides a promising solution to the aforementioned issues. Blockchain is a novel data storage technology, which is built upon decentralized peer-to-peer networks[14]. On a blockchain, each participant is allowed to view the content in all blocks. When a new block is created, the transactions or information that belongs to the corresponding time slot is stored in that block, and all the participant can verify the content in the block. With different mechanisms such as Proof of Work (PoW) and smart contract, blockchain has successfully provided security and privacy for many applications, particularly for cryptocurrencies. However, how to exploit blockchain technology to design secure and privacy-aware applications for ICVs is still a challenging problem due to different security and privacy requirements in such systems. In the literature, there have been a few works on blockchain based ICV applications. For example, Li et al.[35] propose a privacy-preserving incentive announcement network called CreditCoin, which motivates the vehicles to share the data including the traffic status. Michelin et al.[43] develop a blockchain based smart transportation architecture named SpeedyChain, that allow smart vehicles to share their data. Hîrtan et al.[23] describe an architecture of the car navigation system in which the personal data is protected. Nevertheless, most previous works introduce Road Side Infrastructure (RSI), security managers, or other third-party authorities to authorize vehicles or verify communication messages, which essentially share the same concerns with the current centralized systems.

In this section, we exploit blockchain to devise a decentralized real-time city-wide traffic information collection system called TrafficChain, which is both secure against malicious attacks on the system and able to protect vehicles' private information. In particular, TrafficChain is featured with a two-layer blockchain architecture as shown in Fig. 1.2, which includes local chains, one for each road

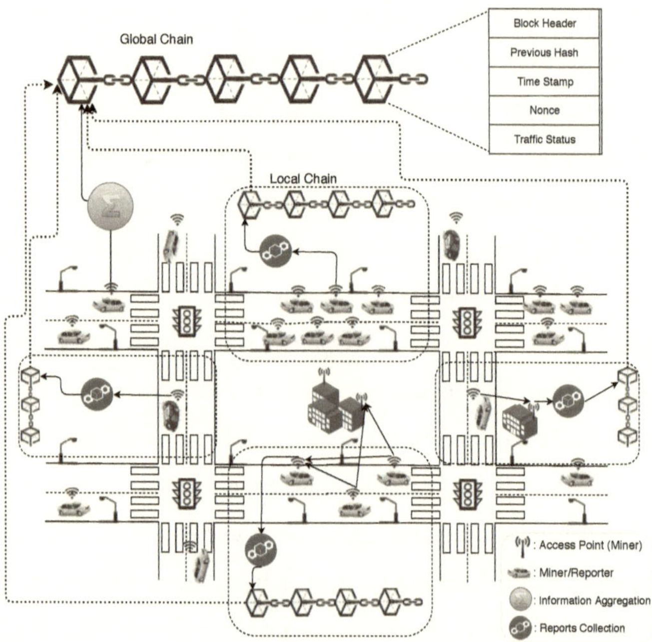

Figure 1.2. A blockchain based secure and privacy-preserving ICV system.

segment, and a global chain. The computing nodes (i.e., "miners") in the system can be either computing nodes owned by individuals (stationary like computers at home and vehicles parked on the streets, or mobile like moving vehicles) that are willing to participate in this system, or edge (or fog) routers that are deployed by "edge service providers (ESP)" providing computing, communication, and storage services for the city, e.g., at the cellular base stations, on the streets, or on top of tall buildings. For each local chain, the "local miners" are the nearby miners who would like to participate. Each block on a local chain is broadcasted to the local miners that are on this particular local chain and all the miners on the global chain. For the global chain, any miner in the city that has enough computing capabilities can be a "global miner". Each block on the global chain contains the aggregated report on the traffic status of each of the road segments and is broadcasted to all the global miners. Whenever a vehicle needs to find a route to some location, it can retrieve the necessary traffic status from the global chain, for example, by inquiring the nearby global miners. In such an architecture, the traffic status collection can be more efficient and the communication overhead can be significantly reduced due to avoiding letting every vehicle broadcast its reports to the whole network.

In addition to a new architecture design, we develop effective algorithms to protect the security of TrafficChain and the privacy of vehicles in the system. We consider Byzantine and Sybil attacks, which are the most popular and challenging attacks to deal with in blockchain based systems. By exploiting a deep learning model called Long Short-Term Memory (LSTM), we design novel LSTM based schemes that can not only defend against Byzantine and Sybil attacks but also make predictions on the forthcoming traffic status in a city. Besides, the SHA256 hash function and Elliptic Curve Digital Signature Algorithm (ECDSA) are employed for generating addresses for each user, where they can generate a large number of addresses for broadcasting reports in different time periods. Thus, the privacy of the participants can be protected.

Our main contributions in blockchain-empowered application are summarized as follows:

- We propose TrafficChain, a blockchain based decentralized real-time traffic information collection system. It has a novel two-layer blockchain architecture that can reduce the network communication overhead and enhance the block update speed, making the system more efficient.

- We introduce the Byzantine attack and Sybil attack on TrafficChain and propose novel LSTM based methods to defend against them. Furthermore, the proposed LSTM based schemes are able to predict the forthcoming traffic status in a city.

- We employ SHA256 and ECDSA to protect users' privacy. With digital signatures and verification schemes, an incentive mechanism is further designed to motivate users to report traffic status in TrafficChain.

- We implement TrafficChain on Ethereum to demonstrate its efficiency and resilience to both Byzantine and Sybil attacks.

2 Literature Review

2.1 Multiparty Learning

Multiparty learning as an emerging topic, many of the related frameworks and applications are proposed. In this section, we explore the extent of these frameworks and technologies.

Yang et al.[72] provide a comprehensive survey of existing works on a secure federated learning framework. Bonawitz et al.[8] build a scalable production system for Federated Learning in the domain of mobile devices. Konečný et al.[30] propose ways to reduce communication costs in federated learning. Nishio and Yonetani[44] propose a new Federated Learning protocol, FedCS, which can actively manage computing workers based on their resource conditions. Zhao et al.[75] notice that conventional federated learning fails on learning non-IID data and propose a strategy to improve training on non-IID data by creating a small subset of data which is globally shared between all the edge devices. Smith et al.[63] propose federated multi-task learning, which is a novel systems-aware optimization method, MOCHA. Besides frameworks, there are many multiparty learning-based applications proposed. De Cock et al.[12] propose a privacy-preserving solution for text classification based on secure multiparty computation, where neither the application nor the text owners learn anything about each other's contents. Shi et al.[60] present a deep sequential model for parsing discourse dependency structures of multi-party dialogues. Ma et al.[40] and Liu et al.[37] consider the traffic trajectories prediction and transportation recommendation based on multiparty learning.

In conventional multiparty learning, a master or a global model is trained based on provided data sources from each party. However, in fact, as learning is becoming more common, each party may be able to train a model (local model) based on their own local data. With conventional multi-party learning, the local models might be ignored, which is a tremendous waste of resources. Targeting this problem, some works are proposed. McMahan et al.[42] advocate to learn a shared model by aggregating local model updates in federated learning, which is proved to be robust to the unbalanced and non-IID data distributions. Shen et al.[59], inspired by Rusu[55], proposed ensemble method (MEAL) distill a variety of trained deep neural networks (DNNs) and transfer to a single DNN. Li et al.[34] propose a byzantine robust stochastic aggregation, which changes the gradient aggregation problem into model aggregation and propose a regularization term in the objective function. Ma et al.[39] propose a protocol for secure multiparty learning (SML) from the aggregation of locally trained models, by using homomorphic proxy re-encryption and aggregate signature techniques. Hamm et al.[20] build an accurate and differentially private global classifier by combining locally-trained classifiers from different parties, without access to any party's private data. Although the above works utilize the local models in multiparty learning, most of them aim to aggregate the local models to a global model and require the local models to be homogeneous. The study on multiparty learning over heterogeneous local models is still limited, where such the case might be more practical in the real application.

Besides, a more general and practical scenario of multiparty learning should be concerned, which is to eliminate the supervision from a central trusted operator. That is to extend multiparty learning to a decentralized network structure. By eliminating the central operator in multiparty learning, the system is resilient from the single point failure, which increases the robustness of multiparty learning. Lalitha et al.[31] consider the problem of training a machine learning model over a network of users in a fully decentralized framework. They propose a decentralized learning algorithm in which users update their belief by aggregate information from their one-hop neighbors to learn a model that best fits the observations over the entire network. Omidshafiei et al.[46] introduce multi-agent reinforcement learning into a decentralized network, where each agent's model variables are distilled into a generalized network.

In decentralized multiparty learning, security and privacy are still the main concern besides the system performance, which is still remaining exploration. Byzantine attacker, who personate honest user and send arbitrary values to others to bias the ultimate system performance, is one of the most common attackers and severely threaten the system reliability. To defend the Byzantine attacks, many works are proposed. Blanchard et al.[6] focus on Byzantine tolerant gradient descent and propose Krum, an aggregation rule that satisfies the resilience property. Wang et al.[67] propose Mean-Around-Krum for secure aggregation in a decentralized traffic system. Chen et al.[11] propose an l-nearest algorithm to defend Byzantine attacks in decentralized Stochastic Gradient Descent (SGD). El-Mhamdi et al.[15] propose

GUANYU, a theoretically proved Byzantine tolerant algorithm on asynchronous networks. Xie et al.[70] explore different aggregation rules for distributed synchronous SGD under a general Byzantine failure model. Regarding security in multiparty learning, several works explore the vulnerabilities of multiparty learning. Mahloujifar et al.[41] show that in a multiparty learning scenario, there always exists an attack (universal poisoning attack) that can increase the probabilities of failure in the master model. Hayes and Ohrimenko[21] show the contamination attacks can taint the model in multiparty learning and present an adversarial training method to against such attacks. Baruch et al.[4] present small but well-crafted changes, called non-omniscient attacks, which are sufficient to attack the central model in distributed learning. Bagdasaryan et al.[3] present a model-poisoning attack that significantly biases the shared model in federated learning. To strengthen the robustness of federated learning, Fung et al.[16], Bonawitz et al.[7], and Liu et al.[38] propose Sybil attack resilient federated learning, secure aggregation protocol in federated learning, and secure federated transfer learning, respectively. Besides, Kairouz et al.[29] study the problem of differential privacy in interactive function computation by multiple parties, where each party wants to compute a function. Although security and privacy problem have been widely studied in multiparty learning, few of them consider the security problem in decentralized multiparty learning with heterogeneous local models. Our work fits in the paradigm of decentralized multiparty learning with heterogeneous models, and further is attack-resilient.

2.2 Traffic Information Collection and Prediction

A big chunk of work exists addressing traffic information collection or prediction in transportation systems. Jabari and Liu[26] propose a stochastic traffic flow model for estimating traffic flow. He and Liu[22] propose a prediction-correction model to describe the traffic equilibration process after an unexpected network disruption. Wang et al.[65] present a NeverStop system, which utilizes genetic algorithms and fuzzy control methods to control the traffic lights at the intersection automatically. Gisdakis et al.[19] leverage state-of-the-art cryptographic schemes and readily available telecommunication infrastructure and present a comprehensive solution to smartphone-based traffic estimation that is proven to be secure and privacy-preserving. Brown et al.[10] introduce Haze, a system that collects traffic statistics from user reports while protecting the users' privacy. Zhu et al.[76] propose a secure and privacy-preserving traffic flow analysis scheme for ICVs, called PTFA, where the traffic information is obtained and aggregated by a traffic regional center through vehicular ad hoc networks (VANETs). Lin et al.[36] identify security and privacy requirements in VANET communications and propose a group signature and identity (ID)-based signature techniques. Rabieh et al.[49] propose privacy-preserving route reporting schemes for traffic management in both infrastructures supported and self-organizing VANETs. Similarly, Zhang et al.[74] propose a privacy-preserving route reporting scheme that only an authenticated vehicle can use the route reporting service provided by the traffic management center. Note that most previous systems assume a trusted central management server, which may not always exist and can be under attacks. A few recent works have employed the blockchain technology to build decentralized ICVs. Rajbhandari et al.[50] examine various blockchain applications in ICVs, and demonstrate that blockchain is applicable and beneficial to the current transportation system. Saranti et al.[56] depict a future of transportation system that combines autonomous vehicle and blockchain. Yuan et al.[73] propose a blockchain based transportation system called La'zooz, which employs a consensus algorithm called proof-of-movement, to generate tokens for ridesharing and other transportation services. Rivera et al.[52] conduct a review for existing research on how to utilize digital identity on the blockchain for ICVs. Pedrosa et al.[48] propose an Ethereum based system to support energy recharges for autonomous electric vehicles. Although these works propose various blockchain based ICV applications, security and privacy in the system are not studied.

Some works address user privacy in ICV applications built on blockchain. Li et al.[35] propose CreditCoin, a privacy-preserving incentive based announcement network on blockchain where users are able to send announcements anonymously in the non-fully trusted environment. Michelin et al.[43] propose a blockchain based smart transportation architecture named SpeedyChain, which ensures reliable Vehicle-to-Infrastructure communication and maintains vehicle privacy by employing periodically changeable keys. Singh et al.[62] propose intelligent vehicles (IV) trust point (IVTP) by using blockchain, aiming at protecting the privacy and security in the communications among vehicles, where every message is signed by the private key of the user. Although a number of works attempt to protect the privacy in ICVs, most of them only focus on the anonymity of the broadcasting messages. Due to the exposure of driving routes for each user, attackers would be able to infer users' identities based on their route information. In our work, we consider the users' driving routes as private information and propose our privacy-preserving method.

Besides, several works are concerned about security issues in ICVs. Su et al.[64] propose an energy blockchain for secure electric vehicles (EV) charging in a smart community, which is to optimally schedule the charging behaviors of EVs with distinct energy consumption preferences. They propose a reputation based Byzantine fault tolerance consensus algorithm. Huang et al.[24] propose a secure decentralized charging pile management system on the blockchain, called lightning network and smart contract (LNSC), which can resist impersonating attack caused by key leaking. Sharma et al.[58] propose a secure and reliable vehicle network architecture based on blockchain, which considers the DoS attack, like jamming on the cloud. Singh et al.[61] propose a trusted environment based Intelligent Vehicle framework, where the blockchain technology provides the trust environment between the vehicles with the based on proof of driving. Lei et al.[33] focus on a critical technique for network security, secure key management scheme, and develop a blockchain based secure key management framework in vehicular communication systems, which can reduce the key transfer time during vehicles handover. Chen et al.[11] target on the Byzantine attacks in a blockchain based distributed systems and propose an l-nearest method to mitigate the attacks. Xie et al.[70] propose three aggregation rules to resist Byzantine attacks in a distributed system, which are respectively based on geometric median, marginal median, and beyond median. Otte et al.[47] propose TrustChain, a Sybil-resistant scalable blockchain, which can determine the trustworthiness of users in order to resist Sybil attacks in a distributed system.

Although cyber-physical attacks like Byzantine and Sybil attacks have been widely studied, many of the methods have high computational complexity and may potentially leak sensitive or private information. Besides, these kinds of attacks have not been fully studied in ICVs. In our TrafficChain, we propose a novel deep learning based secure aggregation scheme that is resilient to both Byzantine and Sybil attacks.

3 Blockchain-Empowered Secure Machine Learning - BEMA

3.1 Problem Formulation

3.1.1 System Overview

We consider that there are N parties in a decentralized learning system. Each party $i \in [1, N]$ has its own local dataset $\mathcal{D}_i = \{\mathcal{X}_i, \mathcal{Y}_i\} = \{(x_i^1, y_i^1), \ldots, (x_i^{n_i}, y_i^{n_i})\}$ containing n_i data samples and their labels. Besides, for any party $i \in [1, N]$, we have $D_i \subset D$, where $\mathcal{D} = \{\mathcal{X}, \mathcal{Y}\}$ is the global dataset and $\mathcal{Y} = \{1, \ldots, C\}$ denotes the set of total C classes. In the learning system, each party i holds a local model f_i that is trained on $\mathcal{D}_i$. Since the classifier f_i is trained on only a partial set of $\mathcal{D}$, it may misclassify an unseen data sample x into a wrong class $y' \in \mathcal{Y}_i$, while its real class is $y \notin \mathcal{Y}_i$. Therefore, each party needs to learn a robust local model that can accurately classify not only unseen data belonging to its learned space, i.e., $y \in \mathcal{Y}_i$ but also data from unknown space, i.e., $y \notin \mathcal{Y}_i$. Particularly, for each party i, its classifier $f_i : \mathcal{X}_i \rightarrow \mathcal{Y}_i$ is obtained by training a local model $\mathcal{M}_i$ with model parameter θ_i, which can be different from those at other parties, e.g., linear regression, Support Vector Machine (SVM), or Artificial Neural Network (ANN). Given a data sample x, the output of f_i is

$$f_i(x) = \arg\max_{y \in \mathcal{Y}_i} h_i(\theta_i, x, y)$$

where $h_i(\theta_i, x, y)$ is a score function for the local model f_i that returns the predicted possibility (or confidence score) of y being the true label of x. Note that $h_i(\theta_i, x, y) = 0$ for $y \notin \mathcal{Y}_i$. In the next few sections, we slightly abuse the notation to use $h_i(x, y)$ or $h_i(\theta_i)$ instead when θ_i or (x, y) is given for brevity.

As shown in Fig. 3.1, a traditional multiparty learning system relies on a central server to coordinate the learning process and calibrate local models, which obviously becomes a single point of failure. Instead, we investigate a blockchain empowered decentralized multiparty learning system without any central server.

A common model calibration method used for multiparty learning with a central server is called multiparty multiclass margin (MPMC-margin)[69]. Before we introduce it, we first present the following definition of the max model predictor.

Definition 1. Max-Model Predictor. Given a set of models $F = \{f_1, \ldots, f_N\}$, the max-model predictor f_F is defined as

$$f_F(x) = \arg\max_{y \in \mathcal{Y}, i \in [1,N]} h_i(x, y).$$

Definition 2. MPMC-margin. For a data sample (x, y), the MPMC-margin is defined as follows

$$\rho(x, y, y^-) = h_a(x, y) - h_b(x, y^-),$$

where y^- is a wrong class label for x, and

$$a = \arg\max_i h_i(x, y), y \in \mathcal{Y}_i,$$

$$b, y^- = \arg\max_{i,y'} h_i(x, y'), y' \in \mathcal{Y}_i \setminus \{y\}.$$

In the MPMC-margin scheme, every party in the learning system has knowledge of all the other parties' current learning models. In each iteration, each party

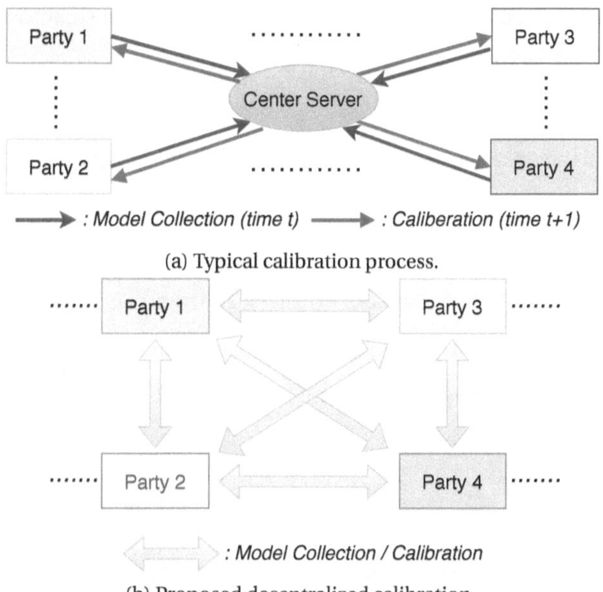

(a) Typical calibration process.

(b) Proposed decentralized calibration.

Figure 3.1. Typical vs. decentralized local model update processes.

exploits its own local data to find a valid calibration sample (x, y, y^-) such that $\rho \leq 0$, and sends the sample to both parties a and b found according to Definition 2. Through different model update methods, party a aims to amplify the importance of (x, y) by increasing $h_a(x, y)$, while party b decreases $h_b(x, y^-)$. After iterations of model calibration, all the parties can update their local models and finally employ the max-model predictor to make classifications.

3.1.2 Threat Model

One of the most common and challenging attacks in decentralized systems is Byzantine attack, where an attacker follows the system protocol but propagates arbitrary malicious information to benign system participants, aiming to degrade the system performance and further mislead or control the system output. The main processes in the proposed system include model collection (i.e., collecting local models from other parties) and model update (i.e., sending calibration messages to particular parties if needed). Correspondingly there exist the following two types of Byzantine attacks.

In type I Byzantine attacks, a malicious party broadcasts a malicious local model to other parties in order to change the classification result of the max-model predictor. Particularly, consider a malicious party $\mathcal{B}$ with a model of $f^{\mathcal{B}}$, where for a sample (x_j, y_j), we have

$$h^{\mathcal{B}}(x_j, y^{\mathcal{B}}) > \max_{i \in \mathcal{H}} h_i(x_j, y_j), \ y^{\mathcal{B}} \in \mathcal{Y}_{\mathcal{B}}.$$

$\mathcal{H}$ is the set of benign parties. In this case, the benign parties that receive the model $f^{\mathcal{B}}$ from party $\mathcal{B}$ will misclassify x_j into a wrong class $y^{\mathcal{B}}$ when applying the max-model predictor.

In type II Byzantine attacks, an attacker $\mathcal{B}$ sends a malicious calibration message to particular parties in order to mislead their local model updating process. For example, suppose that the attacker $\mathcal{B}$ is able to find a class y^- based on its private sample (x, y), where

$$\rho(x, y^-, y) = h_a(x, y^-) - h_b(x, y) < 0, y^- \in \mathcal{Y}_a, y \in \mathcal{Y}. \tag{3.1}$$

Then, the attacker $\mathcal{B}$ can send a malicious calibration message (x, y^-, y) to both parties a and b, so that they will be misled to increase the prediction score on the wrong class and lower the prediction score on the right class, respectively.

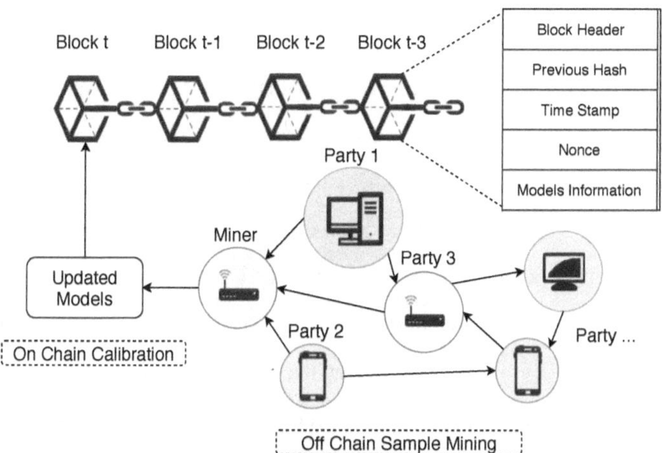

Figure 3.2. The architecture of blockchain-empowered secure multiparty learning.

3.2 Blockchain-Empowered Secure Multiparty Learning (BEMA)

Given the threat model described above, the main challenges in building decentralized multiparty learning are first, to verify the truthfulness of the broadcasted local models of each party, which can affect the max model predictor's output, and second, to verify the truthfulness of the calibration messages, which is critical for updating the local models. To address these challenges, we propose a blockchain-empowered secure multiparty learning system called BEMA, which is detailed in the following.

3.2.1 System Architecture

The main architecture of BEMA is shown in Fig. 3.2. In the system, each party could be an association/institution, or a personal device, like a smartphone or a personal computer. Each party holds a local model, which is trained on its private dataset. As the local models are heterogeneous, the blockchain stores model information, including model type, model parameter, and learned classes. In each time slot, each party can test the models on the chain and search for a valid calibration data sample (x, y, y^-) in its own dataset. If a valid sample is found, each party can broadcast it to the blockchain and win certain system rewards once a miner uses it to update models on the chain. This process is called "off-chain sample mining". The miners in the system collect the calibration samples broadcasted by the learning parties and check the validity of them based on our designed protocol. Once a sample is validated by the miner who wins the authority to write the next block, the miner uses it to update models on the chain, which is called the calibration process. Based on different pre-defined model updating protocols, the miner computes updated model information, constructs a legal block header, and creates a new block. All of the sample validation, calibration, and block construction processes are called "on-chain mining". Note that all the processes in on-chain mining are carefully designed, which will be described next. Furthermore, system rewards can be provided by system initializers, e.g., hospitals that would like to obtain better learning models for medical applications. Since the model update information stored in a block can be viewed and verified by each system participant, the miners, including both off-chain and on-chain ones, can obtain rewards as the new block is built.

3.2.2 System Entities

There are three types of participants in the system, which are the original party, regular party, and miner. The details of their roles are given as follows.

Original Party (OP). The OPs are the parties or associations that start the blockchain. Each OP has its local model and intends to work with each other to learn better local models without directly sharing all its local data. All the OPs are considered to be honest in the system.

Regular Party (RP). The RPs are the participants of the system after the initialization. The same as the OPs, each RP owns a local model trained on its own dataset. The number of OPs and their data amount could be limited. As more RPs join the system, they can help the system learn more robust local models for each party and enable all parties to perform more accurate classifications on the data from unseen classes. RPs are not trustworthy and can potentially launch attacks on the system.

Miner. A miner's main job is to build blocks on the blockchain based on the consensus protocol. Here, we adopt Proof-of-Work[17] as the system consensus protocol. A miner could be either an OP/RP with sufficient computing resources, or an edge device.

3.2.3 Secure Multiparty Learning

BEMA mainly consists of system initialization, off-chain sample mining, and on-chain mining. In system initialization, the OPs register their identities (IDs) and model information on the chain. Afterward, the participating RPs can register their IDs and model information on the chain. The model calibration process is mostly the off-chain and on-chain mining. The former is to find eligible data samples for model calibration, while the latter is to calibrate specific local models based on the found samples and record them in the new blocks. More details are given as follows.

Initialization. For blockchain initialization, consider there are a total of $M(M < N)$ OPs, each of whom holds a local model $h_{Y_i}^{OP}$, where $i \in [1, M]$, $Y_i \subset \mathcal{Y}$. Here, h_{Y_i} represents the model trained on the data from classes of Y_i. Each OP i broadcasts its model information along with its ID, i.e., $\{h_{Y_i}^{OP}, Y_i, ID_{OP_i}\}$. Thus, the first block contains the model information from all OPs, which is

$$< \{h_{Y_1}^{OP}, Y_1, ID_{OP_1}\} \dots, \{h_{Y_M}^{OP}, Y_M, ID_{OP_M}\} > .$$

Denote the set of RPs by $\mathcal{R} = \{1, 2, \dots, R\}$. Each RP needs to have its local model verified by the chain before it can register its model on the chain. Particularly, for a new participant RP j owning data from classes of $Y_j (j \in \mathcal{R})$ and has trained a local model $h_{Y_j}^{RP}$, any OP i with $Y_j \subset Y_i$ can validate RP j's model by checking if the following holds

$$\sum_{(x,y) \in \mathcal{D}_{OP_j}} |h_{Y_j}^{RP}(x, y) - h_{Y_i}^{OP}(x, y)| \le \omega, \tag{3.2}$$

where ω is a pre-defined threshold. If the above condition holds, the OP will sign the approval for initializing the model $h_{Y_j}^{RP}$ for RP j on the chain. Then, a message $< h_{Y_j}^{RP}, ID_{RP_j}, Sign_{OP_i} >$ is broadcasted, which will be included in the new block on the chain. Otherwise, RP j's model is considered to be unqualified for classifying on Y_j, and cannot be registered in the system.

Off-Chain Sample Mining. In off-chain sample mining, each party in the system is encouraged to exploit the local models on the chain with their own dataset, aiming to find a data sample that can help calibrate some of the models. Different from the original MPMC-margin, we propose "secure MPMC-margin" for decentralized systems, which can help defend against Byzantine attacks.

Definition 3. Secure MPMC-margin. For a data sample (x, y), the secure MPMC-margin is defined as follows

$$\rho(x, y, y^-) = h_{a^*}(x, y) - h_{b^*}(x, y^-), y^- \in \mathcal{Y} \setminus \{y\}, \tag{3.3}$$

$$h_{a^*}(x, y) = \frac{1}{m} \sum_{k \xrightarrow{m} a} h_k(x, y), \tag{3.4}$$

$$h_{b^*}(x, y^-) = \frac{1}{m} \sum_{k \xrightarrow{m} b} h_k(x, y^-), \tag{3.5}$$

$$a = \arg\min_{j \in \mathcal{S}(y)} \sum_{k \xrightarrow{m} j} |h_k(x, y) - h_j(x, y)|, \tag{3.6}$$

$$y^- = \arg\max_{y' \in \mathcal{Y} \setminus \{y\}} h_i(x, y'), \tag{3.7}$$

$$i = \arg\min_{j \in \mathcal{S}(y')} \sum_{k \xrightarrow{m} j} |h_k(x, y') - h_j(x, y')|, \tag{3.8}$$

$$b = \arg\min_{j \in \mathcal{S}(y^-)} \sum_{k \xrightarrow{m} j} |h_k(x, y^-) - h_j(x, y^-)|. \tag{3.9}$$

Here, $k \xrightarrow{m} j$ means the m closest value to $h_j(\cdot, \cdot)$, where m equals to $\alpha|\mathcal{S}(y)|$ and $\alpha|\mathcal{S}(y^-)|$ in Eq. (3.6) and Eq. (3.7), respectively. $\mathcal{S}(y)$ and $\mathcal{S}(y^-)$ represent the set of parties that hold data in class y and in class y^-, respectively. $\alpha(0 < \alpha \le 1)$ is a control parameter.

In the original MPMC-margin given in Definition 2, only two models, a and b, are selected to calculate the margin, which get further updated during the calibration process. However, this may not be appropriate in a decentralized system for two reasons. First, as there might be malicious parties in the system, only selecting two models may make the margin calculation process subject to attacks and compromise benign models. Second, based on the original MPMC-margin, only two models are updated in each calibration round, which would be inefficient in a large-scale system. In contrast, in secure MPMC-margin, we adopt the Krum function[6] in Eq. (3.6) and Eq. (3.7) to mitigate the influences from malicious models. Note that, the amount of samples needed for updating all the models is strictly limited as shown in[69], where a small budget (less than 1% of the global data) is sufficient to reach satisfactory results in the experiments.

On-Chain Mining. As mentioned above, each broadcasted sample (x, y, y^-) needs to be validated by the miner and then used for model calibration.

Sample Validation. For a received calibration sample (x, y, y^-), the miner checks its validity by

$$\rho(x, y, y^-) \leq 0, \tag{3.10}$$

$$h_{a^*}(x, y) \geq \delta, \tag{3.11}$$

$$\max_{k \xrightarrow{m} a} |h_k(x, y) - h_{a^*}(x, y)| \leq \sigma, \tag{3.12}$$

where δ and σ are predefined thresholds. Eq. (3.10) assures that (x, y, y^-) is eligible for calibration. Eq. (3.11) and Eq. (3.12) quantify the confidence level that the sample x belongs to class y. If all the above constraints are satisfied, the miner adopts the sample for model calibration.

Model Calibration. With a valid calibration sample (x, y, y^-), the miner updates the corresponding models, particularly their model parameters θ_i's, on the chain. The calibration process may vary for different models due to their heterogeneity. We assume that the models support online update, which is the case for most popular learning models such as linear regression, SVM, and ANN. We also assume that the score functions $h_i(\cdot, \cdot, \cdot)(i \in [1, N])$ are continuously differentiable (we use $h_i(\theta_i)$ in the following to simplify notations). The miner performs $enhance(x, y)$ and

$impair(x, y^-)$ functions on $\mathcal{S}(y)$ and $\mathcal{S}(y^-)$ models that need to be updated by employing the gradient descent method[9,11,53]. Note that the same as in our previous work[11], we put a cap $G(G > 0)$ on the gradient to avoid the gradient exploding problem, i.e.,

$$\Delta_i(\theta_i^t) = \Delta_i(\theta_i^t) / \max(1, \frac{||\Delta_i(\theta_i^t)||_2}{G}).$$

Specifically, the $enhance(x, y)$ function is defined as

$$\forall h_i(x, y) < h_{a^*}(x, y), i \in \mathcal{S}(y),$$

$$\theta_i^{t+1} = \theta_i^t + \eta\Delta_i(\theta_i^t), \tag{3.13}$$

where $\eta > 0$ is a learning rate, and $t + 1$ and t represent after and before update, respectively. This function aims to increase the prediction score of (x, y) for the corresponding models.

Similarly, the $impair(x, y^-)$ function is defined as

$$\forall h_i(x, y^-) > h_{b^*}(x, y^-), i \in \mathcal{S}(y^-),$$

$$\theta_i^{t+1} = \theta_i^t - \eta\Delta_i(\theta_i^t), \tag{3.14}$$

which aims to decrease the prediction score of (x, y^-) for the corresponding models.

Block Creation. The structure of the blocks is shown in Fig. 3.3. For each received valid calibration sample, the miner updates the corresponding models and writes the updated model information in the created block, where the information includes the ID of the party that the model belongs to, the type of the model, model parameters θ, and the used calibration sample (x, y, y^-). The model information is

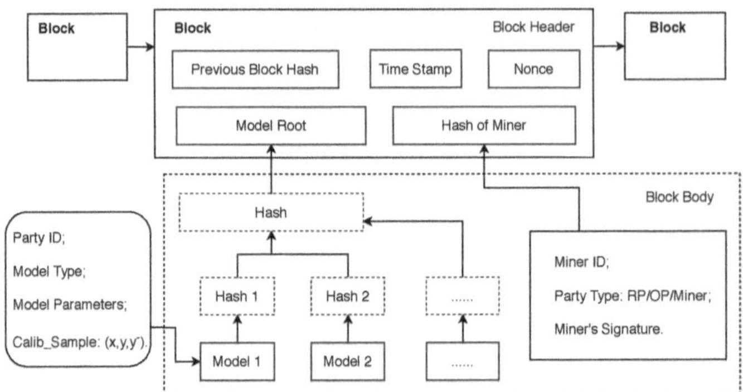

Figure 3.3. The structure of blocks.

stored in a Merkle tree[5] using a double SHA256[18]. Besides, the miner also uploads its own information into the block, including its ID and party type (RP/OP/Miner), by using a double SHA-256. Thus, previous block's hash, time stamp, a nonce, the Merkle tree root, and the hash of the miner's information are included in the block header.

We summarize the main processes of the proposed BEMA system in Algorithm 1.

3.2.4 Krum based Model Predictor

After the above secure multiparty learning, each OP/RP can use the models on the chain to classify unseen data samples. A common method is to apply the max-model predictor given in Definition 1. However, as the max-model predictor finally only selects a single model for classification, such a regular max-model predictor

---

Algorithm 1 Blockchain-empowered Secure Multiparty Learning (BEMA)

1: **Model initialization:**
2: Each OP i broadcasts its model information along with its ID, i.e., $\{h_{Y_i}^{OP}, Y_i, ID_{OP_i}\}$ so as to build the first block.
3: Each RP j broadcasts its local model $h_{Y_j}^{RP}$ to OPs.
4: The OPs check the validity of received models based on Eq. (3.2), and broadcast approval messages $< h_{Y_j}^{RP}, ID_{RP_j}, Sign_{OP_i} >$ that will be included in the next block.
5: **Off-Chain mining:**
6: Each OP/RP finds a valid calibration sample (x, y, y^-) based on Eq. (3.3)-Eq. (3.7).
7: Each OP/RP broadcasts the found calibration sample (x, y, y^-).
8: **On-Chain mining:**
9: Sample validation.
10:    The miner validates each received data sample (x, y, y^-) based on Eq. (3.10)-Eq. (3.12).
11: Model calibration.
12:    The miner updates the corresponding models on the blockchain based on Eq. (3.13) and Eq. (3.14).
13: Block creation.
14:    The miner builds a new block as shown in Fig. 3.3.
15:    The miner broadcasts the new block.

---

may fail in the scenario that not every model in the system is trustworthy. Therefore, we propose the following Krum based model predictor, which exploits all the related models for an unseen data sample in order to give a reliable result.

Definition 4. Krum Based Model Predictor. Given a set of model $F = \{f_1, \ldots, f_N\}$, the Krum based model predictor f_{Krum} is defined as

$$f_{Krum}(x) = \arg\max_{y \in \mathcal{Y}} h_i(x, y), \tag{3.15}$$

$$i = \arg\min_{j \in \mathcal{S}(y)} \sum_{k \xrightarrow{m} j} |h_k(x, y) - h_j(x, y)|. \tag{3.16}$$

3.2.5 System Analysis

Performance Analysis. We present the following theorem to provide insight into the efficacy of our secure multiparty learning process.

Theorem 1. *Assume that 1) each model $h_i(\theta_i)(i \in [1, N])$ is convex, continuously differentiable, and $c_i - lipschitz(c_i > 0)$, and 2) $p_i \leq |\nabla h_i(\theta_i)| \leq b_i$. The secure MPMC-margin improvement after sample calibration at time slot t is bounded by*

$$\frac{2\eta}{m} \min_{i\in[1,N]} \{p_i^2\} \leq \rho^{t+1} - \rho^t \leq$$

$$2\eta \max_{i\in[1,N]} \{c_i\} \min\{ \max_{i\in[1,N]} \{b_i\}, G\}. \tag{3.17}$$

PROOF. For brevity, we rewrite secure MPMC-margin in Eq. (3.3) into the following form at time slot t

$$\rho^t = h_{a^*}^t - h_{b^*}^t.$$

The improvement after sample calibration at time slot t is

$$\rho^{t+1} - \rho^t = (h_{a^*}^{t+1} - h_{a^*}^t) + (h_{b^*}^t - h_{b^*}^{t+1}),$$

where the first term and the second term correspond to the *enhance* and *impair* processes, respectively.

First, we consider the *enhance* process. According to Eq. (3.13), for $h_i(\cdot)$ where $i \in \mathcal{S}(y)$, given a calibration sample (x, y, y^-), we have

$$h_i^{t+1} - h_i^t \geq \nabla h_i(\theta^t)(\theta_i^{t+1} - \theta_i^t)$$

$$= \eta(\nabla h_i(\theta^t))^2,$$

due to the convexity of $h_i(\cdot)$. Besides, since $h_i(\theta_i)$ is $c_i - Lipschitz$, we have

$$h_i^{t+1} - h_i^t \leq c_i|\theta_i^{t+1} - \theta_i^t| = c_i\eta|\nabla h_i(\theta_i^t)|$$

$$\leq c_i\eta \min_{i\in[1,N]} \{b_i, G\}.$$

Similarly, for the *impair* process, for $h_i(\cdot)$ where $i \in \mathcal{S}(y^-)$, we get

$$h_i^t - h_i^{t+1} \geq \eta(\nabla h_i(\theta_i^t))^2$$

$$h_i^t - h_i^{t+1} \leq c_i\eta \min_{i\in[1,N]} \{b_i, G\}.$$

Note that at least one model, say $h_j(\cdot)(j \in \mathcal{S}(y))$, gets enhanced based on the criterion in Eq. (3.13), and at least one model, say $h_k(\cdot)(k \in \mathcal{S}(y^-))$, gets impaired based on the criterion in Eq. (3.14). Therefore, we can obtain

$$h_{a^*}^{t+1} \geq \frac{1}{m}(\sum_{i\in M_a} h_i^t + \eta(\nabla h_j(\theta_j^t))^2) = h_{a^*}^t + \frac{\eta}{m}(\nabla h_j(\theta_j^t))^2,$$

$$h_{b^*}^{t+1} \leq \frac{1}{m}(\sum_{i\in M_b} h_i^t - \eta(\nabla h_k(\theta_k^t))^2) = h_{b^*}^t - \frac{\eta}{m}(\nabla h_k(\theta_k^t))^2,$$

where M_a and M_b represent the set of M models used for calculating $h_{a^*}^t$ and for calculating $h_{b^*}^t$, respectively.

Consequently, we get

$$\rho^{t+1} - \rho^t \geq \frac{\eta}{m}(\nabla h_j(\theta_j^t))^2 + \frac{\eta}{m}(\nabla h_k(\theta_k^t))^2$$

$$\geq \frac{2\eta}{m} \min_{i \in [1,N]} \{p_i^2\}.$$

Moreover, note that at most all models in $\mathcal{S}(y)$ get enhanced and at most all models in $\mathcal{S}(y^-)$ get impaired. Thus, we get

$$h_{a^*}^{t+1} \leq \frac{1}{m}\big(\sum_{i \in M_a} (h_i^t + c_i\eta|\nabla h_i(\theta_i^t)|)\big)$$

$$= h_{a^*}^t + \frac{\eta}{m} \sum_{i \in M_a} c_i|\nabla h_i(\theta_i^t)|$$

$$\leq h_{a^*}^t + \frac{\eta}{m} \max_{i \in [1,N]} \{c_i\} \cdot m \cdot \min\{\max_{i \in [1,N]} \{b_i\}, G\}$$

$$= h_{a^*}^t + \eta \max_{i \in [1,N]} \{c_i\} \min\{\max_{i \in [1,N]} \{b_i\}, G\},$$

$$h_{b^*}^{t+1} \geq \frac{1}{m}\big(\sum_{i \in M_b} (h_i^t - c_i\eta|\nabla h_i(\theta_i^t)|)\big)$$

$$\geq h_{b^*}^t - \eta \max_{i \in [1,N]} \{c_i\} \min\{\max_{i \in [1,N]} \{b_i\}, G\}.$$

Consequently, we have

$$\rho^{t+1} - \rho^t \leq 2\eta \max_{i \in [1,N]} \{c_i\} \min\{\max_{i \in [1,N]} \{b_i\}, G\}.$$

$\square$

Security Analysis. As we mentioned in Section 3.1.2, there are two types of Byzantine attacks in decentralized multiparty learning. For type I Byzantine attacks, we take advantage of the OPs to validate each RP's model as shown in Eq. (3.2). The control parameter ω indicates the requirement on the model of RP j requesting to join the system. In particular, RP j's model, i.e., $h_{Y_j}^{RP}$, is required to perform similarly to the corresponding OP's local models that include Y_j in their learning spaces.

Furthermore, with the designed blockchain based multiparty learning system, the model updating process is public and can be verified by all the participants on the blockchain. Thus, the system can ensure the validity of each model's updating process, even though the newly registered RP's model is, to some extent, malicious at the beginning.

Type II Byzantine attacks are another main security concern of the proposed system, where the bogus calibration sample may severely disrupt the model update process. We show that the proposed secure MPMC-margin has bounded performance under type II Byzantine attacks in following theorems.

Theorem 2. *Consider the set of models $S(y) = \{h_1, \ldots, h_{|S(y)|}\}$ that aim to classify data in class y. Let $|S(y)| = K^{S(y)} + f^{S(y)}$, where $K^{S(y)}$ and $f^{S(y)}$ represent the number of honest models and that of malicious models, respectively. Assume $2f^{S(y)} < m < K^{S(y)}$, where m is defined in Definition 3. Given a data example (x, y), let $h_{min}(x, y)$ and $h_{max}(x, y)$ denote the minimum and maximum output of honest models, respectively. Then, $h_{a^*}(x, y)$ in Eq. (3.4) in the worst case is bounded by*

$$h_{min}(x, y) - \frac{f^{S(y)}}{m}(h_{max}(x, y) - h_{min}(x, y)) < h_{a^*}(x, y)$$

$$< h_{max}(x, y) + \frac{f^{S(y)}}{m}(h_{max}(x, y) - h_{min}(x, y)). \tag{3.18}$$

Similarly, consider the set of models $S(y^-)$ that aim to classify data in class y^-. Given data sample (x, y^-), $h_{b^*}(x, y)$ in Eq. (3.5) in the worst case is bounded by

$$h_{min}(x, y^-) - \frac{f^{S(y^-)}}{m}(h_{max}(x, y^-) - h_{min}(x, y^-))$$

$$< h_{b^*}(x, y) <$$

$$h_{max}(x, y^-) + \frac{f^{S(y^-)}}{m}(h_{max}(x, y^-) - h_{min}(x, y^-)). \tag{3.19}$$

PROOF. We present the proof for Eq. (3.18) in the following, while the proof for Eq. (3.19) directly follows. To simplify the notations, we omit the subscripts and superscripts in $K^{S(y)}$ and $f^{S(y)}$.

Let $H^B = \{h_1^B, \ldots, h_f^B\}$ denote all the byzantine models (malicious models) in $S(y)$, where $h_l^B(x, y) \leq h_{l+1}^B(x, y), l \in [1, f - 1]$, and $H^O = \{h_1^O, \ldots, h_K^O\}$ denote all the honest models in $\mathcal{S}(y)$, where $h_l^{\mathcal{O}}(x, y) \leq h_{l+1}^{\mathcal{O}}(x, y), l \in [1, K - 1]$. Thus, we have $\{h_{min}, h_{max}\} = \{h_1^{\mathcal{O}}, h_K^{\mathcal{O}}\}$.

To analyze the bounds of Eq. (3.4) in the worst case, we consider the scenario where all the Byzantine models are included in the aggregation. So, Eq. (3.4) can be rewritten into

$$h_{a^*} = \frac{1}{m}\left(\sum_i^f h_i^{\mathcal{B}} + \sum_j^{m-f} h_j^{\mathcal{O}}\right).$$

Besides, the ground truth is $\frac{1}{K}\sum_{i=1}^K h_i^{\mathcal{O}} \in [h_{min}, h_{max}]$, while the second term in h_{a^*} is $\sum^{m-f} h_j^{\mathcal{O}} \in [(m - f)h_{min}, (m - f)h_{max}]$. Since we have $m > 2f$, although all malicious models are included in the aggregation, h_a is still located in $[h_{min}, h_{max}]$ according to Eq. (3.6). The proof of this is given in Lemma 1 in the following.

The objective of attackers is to steer the aggregated value h_{a^*} as small or large as possible. Therefore, we discuss the attack in two worst cases.

Case I: All the malicious models aim to steer h_{a^*} smaller, where $h_f^{\mathcal{B}} < h_{min} \leq h_a$. From Eq. (3.6), we get

$$|h_1^{\mathcal{B}} - h_a| + \cdots + |h_f^{\mathcal{B}} - h_a| + |h_1^{\mathcal{O}} - h_a| + \ldots$$
$$+ |h_{m-f}^{\mathcal{O}} - h_a| <$$
$$|h_{m-f+1}^{\mathcal{O}} - h_a| + \cdots + |h_m^{\mathcal{O}} - h_a| + |h_1^{\mathcal{O}} - h_a| + \ldots$$
$$+ |h_{m-f}^{\mathcal{O}} - h_a|.$$

Due to $h_f^{\mathcal{B}} < h_a < h_{m-f+1}^{\mathcal{O}}$, the above inequality can be rewritten into

$$f h_a - \sum_{l=1}^f h_l^{\mathcal{B}} < \sum_{l=m-f+1}^m h_l^{\mathcal{O}} - f h_a$$

$$\Rightarrow \sum_{l=1}^f h_l^{\mathcal{B}} > 2f h_a - \sum_{l=m-f+1}^m h_l^{\mathcal{O}} > 2f h_{min} - f h_{max}$$

$$\Rightarrow \sum_{l=1}^f h_l^{\mathcal{B}} + \sum_{l=1}^{m-f} h_l^{\mathcal{O}} > 2f h_{min} - f h_{max} + (m - f)h_{min}$$

$$= (m + f)h_{min} - f h_{max}$$

$$\Rightarrow h_{a^*} > h_{min} - \frac{f}{m}(h_{max} - h_{min}). \tag{3.20}$$

Case II: All the malicious models aim to steer h_{a^*} greater, where $h_1^{\mathcal{B}} > h_{max} \geq h_a$. Similarly, we get

$$|h_1^{\mathcal{B}} - h_a| + \cdots + |h_f^{\mathcal{B}} - h_a| +$$

$$|h_{K-m+f+1}^{\mathcal{O}} - h_a| + \cdots + |h_K^{\mathcal{O}} - h_a| <$$

$$|h_{K-m+1}^{\mathcal{O}} - h_a| + \cdots + |h_{K-m+f}^{\mathcal{O}} - h_a| +$$

$$|h_{K-m+f+1}^{\mathcal{O}} - h_a| + \cdots + |h_K^{\mathcal{O}} - h_a|.$$

Because of $h_1^{\mathcal{B}} > h_a > h_{K-m+f}^{\mathcal{O}}$, we have

$$\sum_{l=1}^{f} h_l^{\mathcal{B}} - f h_a < f h_a - \sum_{l=K-m+1}^{K-m+f} h_l^{\mathcal{O}}$$

$$\Rightarrow \sum_{l=1}^{f} h_l^{\mathcal{B}} < 2 f h_a - \sum_{l=K-m+1}^{K-m+f} h_l^{\mathcal{O}} < 2 f h_{max} - f h_{min}$$

$$\Rightarrow \sum_{l=1}^{f} h_l^{\mathcal{B}} + \sum_{l=K-m+f+1}^{K} h_l^{\mathcal{O}} < 2 f h_{max} - f h_{min}$$

$$+(m-f) h_{max} = (m+f) h_{max} - f h_{min}$$

$$\Rightarrow h_{a^*} < h_{max} + \frac{f}{m}(h_{max} - h_{min}). \tag{3.21}$$

Thus, we arrive at Eq. (3.18) and Eq. (3.19) directly follows. $\qquad\square$

Lemma 1. *Under the same conditions as in Theorem 2, in the worst case that all Byzantine reports are included in the aggreggation, we have $h_a \in [h_{min}, h_{max}]$.*

PROOF. Note that $h_{min} = h_1^{\mathcal{O}}$ and $h_{max} = h_K^{\mathcal{O}}$. We first consider the worst case that the Byzantine attackers aim to maliciously make h_a very small, where $h_f^{\mathcal{B}} < h_{min}$. Thus, the report set of "$k \xrightarrow{m} j$" in Eq. (3.6) can be written as $\mathbf{h} = \{h_1, h_2, \ldots, h_m\} = \{h_1^{\mathcal{B}}, \ldots, h_f^{\mathcal{B}}, h_1^{\mathcal{O}}, \ldots, h_{(m-f)}^{\mathcal{O}}\}$.

Define $KR(j) = \sum_{k \xrightarrow{m} j} |h_k - h_j|$ and $\Delta_{ij} = |h_i - h_j|$. Then, we have

$$KR(s) = \Delta_{1s} + \cdots + \Delta_{(s-1)s} +$$

$$\Delta_{(s+1)s} + \cdots + \Delta_{ms},$$

$$KR(s+1) = \Delta_{1(s+1)} + \cdots + \Delta_{s(s+1)} +$$

$$\Delta_{(s+2)(s+1)} + \cdots + \Delta_{m(s+1)}.$$

Note that $\Delta_{i(s+1)} = \Delta_{is} + \Delta_{s(s+1)}$ for $1 \leq i < s$ and $\Delta_{i(s+1)} = \Delta_{is} - \Delta_{s(s+1)}$ for $s + 1 < i \leq m$. Thus, we can obtain

$$
\begin{aligned}
KR(s+1) =& \Delta_{1s} + \Delta_{2s} + \cdots + \Delta_{(s-1)s} + \\
& (s-1)\Delta_{s(s+1)} + \Delta_{s(s+1)} + \Delta_{(s+2)s} \\
& + \cdots + \Delta_{ms} - (m-s-1)\Delta_{s(s+1)} \\
=& KR(s) + (2s - m)\Delta_{s(s+1)}.
\end{aligned}
$$

Due to $m \geq 2f$, we have $KR(s+1) < KR(s)$ for $1 \leq s \leq f$, which means $KR(f+1) < KR(f)$. Consequently, we get $h_a \geq h_{min}$.

Similarly, in the worst case that Byzantine attackers aim to maliciously make h_a very large, where $h_1^{\mathcal{B}} > h_{max}$, we can prove that $h_a \leq h_{max}$.

Therefore, Lemma 1 follows.

$\square$

Theorem 3. *Under the same assumptions as in Theorem 2, the secure MPMC-margin $\rho(x, y, y^-)$ in Eq. (3.3) is bounded by*

$$
h_{min}(x, y) - h_{max}(x, y^-) - \frac{f^{\mathcal{S}(y)}}{m}(h_{max}(x, y) - h_{min}(x, y))
$$

$$
- \frac{f^{\mathcal{S}(y^-)}}{m}(h_{max}(x, y^-) - h_{min}(x, y^-)) < \rho(x, y, y^-) <
$$

$$
h_{max}(x, y) - h_{min}(x, y^-) + \frac{f^{\mathcal{S}(y)}}{m}(h_{max}(x, y) - h_{min}(x, y))
$$

$$
+ \frac{f^{\mathcal{S}(y^-)}}{m}(h_{max}(x, y^-) - h_{min}(x, y^-)). \tag{3.22}
$$

PROOF. According to Eq. (3.18), Eq. (3.19), and Eq. (3.3), we arrive at Theorem 3.

$\square$

4 Blockchain-Empowered Smart Transportation - TrafficChain

4.1 Problem Formulation

In this chapter, we first introduce some preliminaries about blockchain. Then, we model the decentralized traffic status collection problem, and describe the corresponding threat models in the system.

4.1.1 Blockchain

Blockchain is a distributed, decentralized, public ledger. Originally devised for financial applications such as cryptocurrencies, the technology has now found use in many other applications such as smart health, smart business, smart city. One of the main features of blockchain is that it provides a decentralized solution to various traditional systems, where all the system information, e.g., transactions in digital currency systems, is stored in blocks and shared among all the participants. With communications through a peer-to-peer network, blockchain is capable of eliminating the need of an authorized third-party, e.g., bank, and hence has no concern about a single point of failure. Furthermore, with the design of different

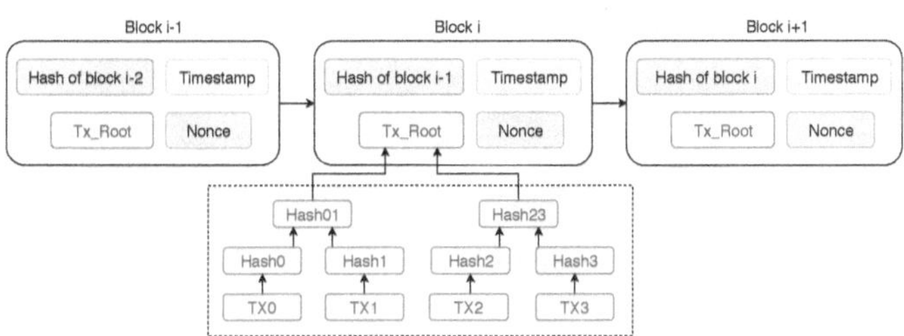

Figure 4.1. The typical blockchain structure.

consensus protocols, e.g. proof of work (PoW) and proof of stake (PoS), blockchain is resilient to dishonest participants.

As shown in Fig. 4.1, blocks on a blockchain are linked chronologically, each of which contains four parts, i.e., the previous block's hash code, time stamp, transaction records, and a nonce. Among them, transaction records are represented by a Merkle tree. The nonce needs to be found by the miners so that the current block's hash fulfills certain system requirement. The miner who finds this nonce first, through PoW, wins the authority to write the new transactions stored in its memory pool into this current block and append it to the chain.

4.1.2 Decentralized Traffic Status Generation

We define city traffic status as the passing time cost for each road segment. Denote the traffic status in the time slot i by $\mathbf{t}_i = [t_i^1, t_i^2, ..., t_i^N]$, where N is the total number of road segments, and t_i^j is the passing time cost for the jth road segment in the time slot i. Suppose that in the time slot i there are h_i^j reports about t_i^j, which are denoted by $\mathbf{t}_i^j = \{t_i^j(k), 1 \leq k \leq h_i^j\}$. To obtain the estimated passing time cost t_i, we design an aggregation function which is represented by $A(\cdot)$. Thus, we have

$$t_i^j = A(t_i^j(1), \ldots, t_i^j(h_i^j)), j \in [1, N]. \tag{4.1}$$

A naive aggregation method is to calculate the average of all reports, which we consider as a benchmark, i.e.,

$$\bar{t}_i^j = \frac{1}{h_i^j} \sum_{k=1}^{h_i^j} t_i^j(k), j \in [1, N]. \tag{4.2}$$

Note that the benchmark may be ineffective, particularly when there are malicious reporters in the system.

4.1.3 Threat Model

We consider the following privacy and security threats in the system.

Privacy. The privacy in the system refers to two types of sensitive information: each user's identity and driving route. A user's identity includes both the driver's identity and the vehicle's identity, both of which need to be protected. Each user's driving route includes the road segments that the user passes through. It is very sensitive information since attackers can infer the user's identity and many details about this user's daily life (such as work location, home address, frequently visited places), and also track the user. Therefore, it is critical to protect each user's privacy in the system.

Security. We are primarily concerned with Byzantine attacks and Sybil attacks in the system, which are described below.

Byzantine attacks. Byzantine attackers report bogus reports in order to disrupt the normal report aggregation process in the system. For example, a Byzantine attacker can report a very high passing time for a certain road segment, which may lead the aggregated passing time to be much higher than it really is, thus forcing other users to use other roads while letting itself go through the road very fast. On the other hand, a Byzantine attacker can report a very low passing time for a road segment, which may mislead other users to use the road segment that is actually already crowded, thus exaggerating the traffic congestion.

Sybil attacks. Sybil attackers can create many different identities in the system in order to disrupt normal system operations. In particular, a Sybil traffic data reporter can use different identities to submit a number of bogus reports for the same road segment to improve the chance that the aggregated passing time for that road segment does get deviated from its true value. Besides, a Sybil miner can take advantage of many different identities to obtain more opportunities of writing blocks on the blockchain.

4.2 TrafficChain: Real-Time Traffic Status Collection on Blockchain

4.2.1 System Overview

In this section, we introduce the proposed real-time traffic status collection system on blockchain, i.e., TrafficChain, in detail. Different from most traditional ICV applications, TrafficChain has a decentralized architecture, which meanwhile is secure and privacy-preserving. The objective of TrafficChain is to securely collect and store the real-time traffic status in a city on the blockchain, which includes the estimated passing time cost for each road segment in the city and can be retrieved by each service demanding vehicle. The computing nodes (i.e., "miners") in the system can be either computing nodes owned by individuals (stationary like computers at home and vehicles parked on the streets, or mobile like moving vehicles), that are willing to participate in this system, or edge (or fog) routers that are deployed by "edge service providers (ESP)" providing computing, communication, and storage services for the city, e.g., at the cellular base stations, on the streets, or on top of tall buildings.

In particular, we propose a two-layer architecture for TrafficChain, which includes local chains, one for each road segment, and a global chain. For each local chain, the "local miners" are the nearby miners who would like to participate in the traffic status collection for the corresponding road segment. Each block on a local chain includes all the reports for the corresponding road segment and is only multicasted to these nearby local miners that are on this particular local chain. For the global chain, all the miners in the city can be the "global miners" for this global chain. Each block on the global chain contains the aggregated report on the traffic status of each of the road segments and is broadcasted to all the global miners. Whenever a vehicle needs to find a route to some location, it can retrieve the necessary traffic status from the global chain, for example, by inquiring the nearby global miners.

Besides, we aim to address the following critical issues in TrafficChain, including preservation of vehicles' privacy, resilience towards the aforementioned two types of attacks, and system anomaly detection. In the following, we first introduce the architecture of the proposed TrafficChain, and then elaborate on the privacy-preserving scheme and the security assuring algorithms.

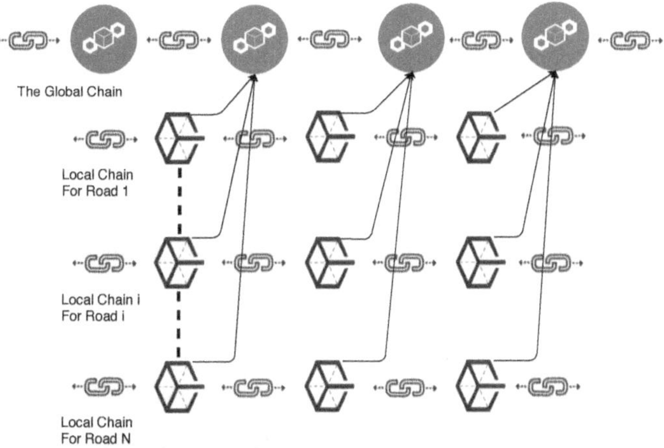

Figure 4.2. The architecture of the TrafficChain.

4.2.2 The Architecture of TrafficChain

The essential information that TrafficChain collects and stores is the passing time cost for each road segment. In general, each vehicle will report the passing time cost for the road segment that it just passed down, while the miner in TrafficChain will aggregate the reports and generate the estimated time cost for each road segment. However, if every vehicle simply broadcasts their reports to all the miners in the city, e.g., through a 5G cellular network or an edge network covering the whole city, the communication network will suffer from very high communication overhead, while every miner will be overloaded with a very high computational burden. Considering this practical issue, we propose a two-layer blockchain architecture for TrafficChain, which includes local chains and a global chain as shown in Fig. 4.2. There is a local chain for each road segment. All the vehicles passing down a road segment will report their individual passing time cost to the corresponding local chain. The local miners compete through Proof-of-Work (PoW) to determine who gets to write the next block containing all the reports from the vehicles. The winning local miner will broadcast the new block to all the miners on the local chain and those on the global chain. After receiving the blocks from the local chains, the global miners employ PoW as the consensus protocol to determine who "mines" the next block containing the traffic status of the city and all the reports from the local miners. The traffic status is obtained based on the local reports, by employing our proposed LSTM based aggregation scheme that will be introduced later.

Block Structures. The structures for the blocks on the local chains and on the global chain are shown in Fig. 4.3 and Fig. 4.4, respectively.

In a local chain block, the block header stores the previous block's hash value, timestamp, a Merkle tree root, and a nonce. In the block body, the data is stored in a Merkle tree. For a local chain j, the data includes aggregated time cost, aggregated reports quantity, all the traffic reports for the corresponding road segment j broadcasted by the passing by vehicles, which are the passing time costs on the road segment j and will be detailed later.

Different from local chains, the global chain contains the global traffic information for the whole city. In a global chain block, the block header has the same structure as that of a local chain block. In the block body, the first element is the city traffic status vector $\mathbf{t}_i$ representing the aggregated time cost for each road in the time slot i, which collected from local miners who aggregate local traffic reports. The second element is $\hat{\mathbf{y}}_{i+1}$, i.e., the predicted traffic status in the next time slot by our proposed time cost estimation LSTM (TE-LSTM), which will be used by the local miners to aggregate local traffic reports in the next time slot. The third

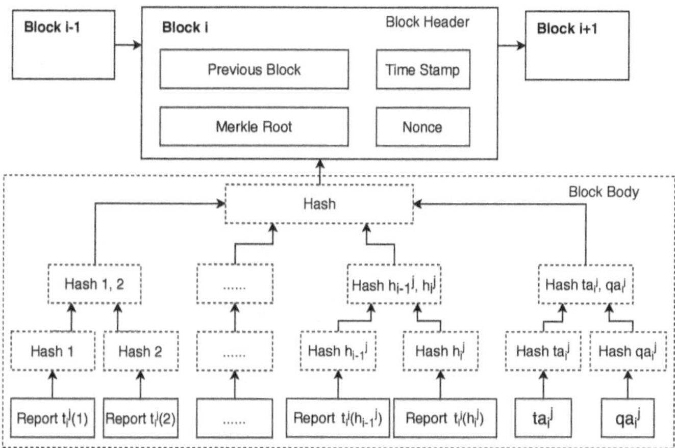

Figure 4.3. The structure of the blocks on local chain j, which is corresponding to road segment j.

element is q_i representing the aggregated traffic report quantity for each road segment. The fourth element is $\hat{y}'_{i+1}$, which is the predicted traffic report quantity for the next time slot. The next elements are the local Merkel trees' roots. Note that every global miner has all the local chains already. Thus, having only the local Merkel trees' roots in the global block is enough and can greatly reduce the size of the global block. The rest two elements are the parameters from our proposed LSTM based aggregation method, i.e., model weights and model gradients, which is used for defending against Byzantine attacks and Sybil attacks. All the above elements are stored in a Merkel tree, whose root is included in the global block header.

The blocks in both local chains and the global chain are chained up chronologically. Each block records the data collected in a time slot, the length of which can be set as needed.

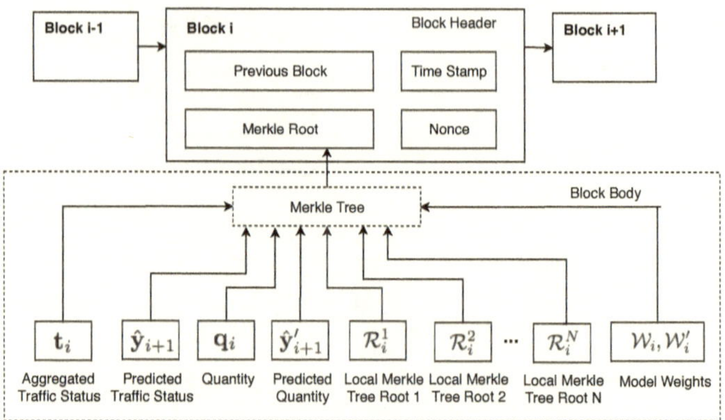

Figure 4.4. The structure of the blocks on the global chain.

Traffic Reporters. In TrafficChain, the traffic reporters typically refer to the vehicles driving in the streets, which are encouraged to report the recorded time cost for the road segments that it has passed down. In the meantime, traffic reporters' privacy as defined in Sec. 4.2.1, i.e., their identities and driving routes, need to be protected.

Towards this goal, each user first generates its own blockchain address, e.g., the SHA256 and RIPEMD160 hash functions on its ECDSA public key like that on the bitcoin blockchain[28]. Note that each user can generate an unlimited number of addresses on a given private key, for example, similar to that in sequential or hierarchical deterministic wallets, and hence use different addresses for reports for different road segments to protect its identity.

The traffic reports are generated as follows. Consider a user k on road segment j in the time slot i. It will first generate a message tuple:

$$m_i^j(k) =< road_j, t_i^j(k), timestamp >, \tag{4.3}$$

where $road_j$ is the ID of the road segment j, $t_i^j(k)$ is the reported passing time cost, *timestamp* represents the time when the report is generated. Next, user k signs the message with a signature $< r_i^j(k), s_i^j(k) >$. Particularly, all users in the system share the same curve parameters $(CURVE, G, n)$, where $CURVE$ is an elliptic curve equation, G is an elliptic curve base point, and n is a prime and the order of G. To generate a signature, the detail process is as follows. User k first generates a private key integer $a \in [1, n-1]$, and a public key with elliptic curve point multiplication, i.e., $b = a \times G$. The signature $< r_i^j(k), s_i^j(k) >$ is generated by

$$r_i^j(k) = x_i^j \bmod n, \tag{4.4}$$

$$s_i^j(k) = R^{-1}(H(m) + r_i^j a), \tag{4.5}$$

respectively. Here, $H(\cdot)$ is the hash function SHA256, R is a secure per message random integer on $[1, n-1]$, x_i^j is from a curve point $(x_i^j, y_i^j) = R \times G$. At last, user k broadcasts the following traffic report to the local miners for the road segment j in the time slot i:

$$\mathcal{R}_i^j(k) =< b^k, r_i^j(k), s_i^j(k), m_i^j(k) > \tag{4.6}$$

where b^k is the address of user k. The process for user k to generate a traffic status report for road segment j in the time slot i is summarized in Algorithm 2.

Algorithm 2 Traffic Report Generation

Input: $CURVE, G, n$, and current time *timestamp*.
    Private key a $1 \le a \le n-1$; public key $b \leftarrow a \times G$.
    TrafficChain address $\leftarrow b$.
    Message $m_i^j(k)$ $< road_j, t_i^j(k), timestamp >$.
    Signature $< r_i^j(k), s_i^j(k) > \leftarrow$ Calculate equations (4) & (5).
    Report $\mathcal{R}_i^j(k)$ $< b^k, r_i^j(k), s_i^j(k), m_i^j(k) >$.
Output: $\mathcal{R}_i^j(k)$.

Note that the public and private keys are utilized for protecting user identities and signing the message, while the messages are not encrypted. Thus, attacks like the Dolev-Yao model[13] are not concerns of our system. Besides, to motivate the users to submit traffic status reports, we design an incentive mechanism for the regular nodes that broadcast traffic status. The details of the incentive mechanism will be detailed later.

Computing Nodes. The computing nodes or miners compete through PoW to win the authority for creating new blocks. As mentioned before, the winning local miner will broadcast the new block to all the miners on the local chain and those on the global chain. After receiving the blocks from the local chains, the global miners also compete through PoW to get to write new blocks on the global chain. The winning global miner employs our proposed LSTM based aggregation algorithms to aggregate all the local reports, which are resilient to Byzantine and Sybil attacks and will be discussed next.

4.2.3 Secure Traffic Report Aggregation on TrafficChain

Recall that the passing time cost reports about each road segments need to be aggregated as shown in Eq. (4.1). How to ensure that the reports aggregation is correct and resilient against both Byzantine attackers and Sybil attackers is a very challenging and critical problem in TrafficChain. In this section, we design a secure aggregation method by utilizing a deep learning model called LSTM.

LSTM Based Secure Report Aggregation. Deep learning techniques, such as Artificial Neural Network (ANN), Recurrent Neural Network (RNN), LSTM, have been widely employed in various applications due to their strong capability in data pattern and correlation mining[27,66]. In TrafficChain, it is obvious that the road passing time cost for and the number of vehicles on each road segment are highly related to the history data on the same road segment and the data on other road segments, which essentially indicates the spatiotemporal correlation among the traffic status data. Therefore, we employ the LSTM model to predict the traffic status and the number of vehicles on all the road segments, which are then used to defend against Byzantine and Sybil attacks. In the following, we describe a Byzantine attack resilient algorithm and a Sybil attack resilient algorithm, respectively, in detail.

A Byzantine Attack Resilient Algorithm. First, we develop a time cost estimation LSTM (TE-LSTM) neural network for global miners to predict the traffic status on all the road segments. In particular, the TE-LSTM network is trained with a data batch denoted by $\mathbf{X} = \{\mathbf{X}_1, \ldots, \mathbf{X}_Q\}$, where $\mathbf{X}_i \in \mathbf{X}$ is a data sample. For each data sample, we have $\mathbf{X}_i = \{\mathbf{ta}_{i-\tau}, \mathbf{ta}_{i-\tau+1}, \ldots, \mathbf{ta}_{i-1}\}(1 \leq i \leq Q)$. Note that $\mathbf{ta} = [ta_i^1, ta_i^2, \ldots, ta_i^N]$ is the aggregated traffic status on all the road segments in the time slot i (ta_i^j represents the aggregated time cost for road segment j in the time slot i and will be introduced later) collected from local miners, τ is the lookback window size representing the amount of temporal information used for each prediction. The structure of the TE-LSTM network is shown in Fig. 4.5. For each data sample $\mathbf{X}_i$, we expect the output of the network $\hat{\mathbf{y}}_i$ to be close to $\mathbf{y}_i = \mathbf{ta}_i$. Particularly, we denote by $G(\cdot)$ the classification function of the proposed TE-LSTM network, and $\mathcal{W}$ the model parameter set that needs to be optimized during the training process. The objective function of TE-LSTM, denoted by $J(\mathcal{W})$, is:

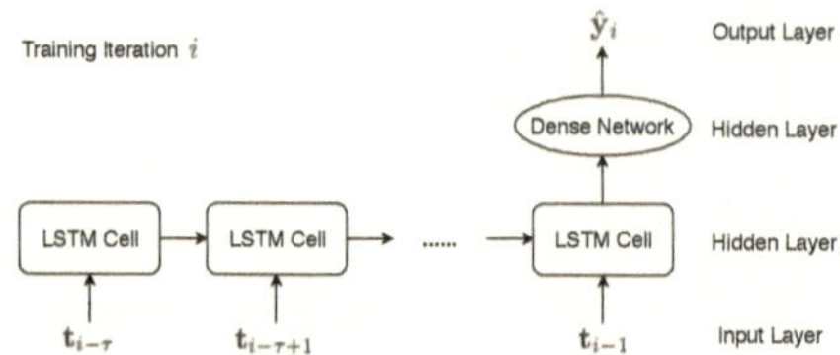

Figure 4.5. The structure of the TE-LSTM network.

$$J(\mathcal{W}) = \frac{1}{Q}\sum_{i=1}^{Q}\phi(G(\mathcal{W};\mathbf{X}_i),\mathbf{y}_i) + \frac{\lambda}{2}||\mathcal{W}||_2^2 \tag{4.7}$$

where $\phi(\cdot)$ is the loss function, $||\mathcal{W}||_2^2$ is the regularization term, and $\lambda > 0$ is the regularization coefficient.

Note that all the global miners share the same TE-LSTM network that can predict the passing time costs on all the road segments in the city. The TE-LSTM network can be trained and initialized by a certain winning global miner using the history traffic status stored on the global chain, and published in the new global block. The winning global miner also predicts the passing time costs on all the road segments in the next time slot based on the TE-LSTM model and writes them in the new global block. In the next time slot, when the winning local miner aggregates the passing time cost reports for the corresponding road segment, it employs the predicted value by the winning global miner in the previous time slot as a reference value.

Second, by taking advantage of the predicted time cost by TE-LSTM, we propose our Byzantine resilient aggregation method based on an existing scheme Krum[6], which is called Mean-Around-Krum. Recall that in the time slot i for road segment j, local miners have the traffic reports by vehicles denoted by $\mathbf{t}_i^j = \{t_i^j(1),\ldots,t_i^j(h_i^j)\}$, where h_i^j is the number of reports that include both honest and bogus reports. The aggregated time cost ta_i^j is calculated as:

$$ta_i^j = (1 - \frac{\mu}{|t_i^{j*} - \hat{y}_i^j|})t_i^{j*} + (\frac{\mu}{|t_i^{j*} - \hat{y}_i^j|})\hat{y}_i^j, \tag{4.8}$$

$$t_i^{j*} = \frac{1}{m} \sum_{k \to k^*} t_i^j(k), \tag{4.9}$$

$$k^* = \underset{I \in [1, h_i^j]}{\operatorname{argmin}} \sum_{p \to I} |t_i^j(p) - t_i^j(I)|. \tag{4.10}$$

Here, $\hat{y}_i^j$ is the estimated time cost given by TE-LSTM from the last time slot $i - 1$, t_i^{j*} is the aggregated value from Mean-Around-Krum method, $k \to j$ means the m closest reported costs to t_j, μ is a control parameter. Particularly, Eq. (4.10) is from the Krum method, which is to find the index of the report that the m closest neighbors have the smallest total distance from. Our final aggregated time cost ta_i^j is a weighted sum of the cost t_i^{j*} given by Mean-Around-Krum and the cost $\hat{y}_i^j$ estimated by TE-LSTM. As t_i^{j*} gets close to $\hat{y}_i^j$, it means that the system is under a regular pattern, and the weight of $\hat{y}_i^j$ is larger. Otherwise, it shows that system may be subject to an abnormal pattern because of sudden changes, e.g., traffic accidents or attacks, and hence the weight of $\hat{y}_i^j$ decreases.

Recall that the winning local miner broadcasts the new local block to all the miners on the local chain and those on the global chain. When a winning global miner gets the authority to write a new global block, it will have the aggregated passing time cost on all the road segments in the current time slot, and utilize this new traffic status data to update the current TE-LSTM model. Specifically, at the end of the ith time slot, the winning global miner can have a new training sample $\mathbf{X}_i = \{\mathbf{ta}_{i-\tau}, \ldots, \mathbf{ta}_{i-1}\}, \mathbf{y}_i = \mathbf{ta}_i$. Then, it employs the Stochastic Gradient Descent (SGD) algorithm to minimize the objective function and in turn update the model parameter set $\mathcal{W}$, where the gradient is calculated as

$$\nabla J(\mathcal{W}_{i-1}) = \frac{d}{d\mathcal{W}_{i-1}}\phi(G(\mathcal{W}_{i-1}; \mathbf{X}_i), \mathbf{y}_i) + \lambda\mathcal{W}_{i-1} \qquad (4.11)$$

Note that the loss function ϕ is considered to be convex and differentiable, e.g., the mean square loss function. Subsequently, the winning global miner updates the model parameter set as follows:

$$\mathcal{W}_i = \mathcal{W}_{i-1} + \eta\nabla J(\mathcal{W}_{i-1}) \qquad (4.12)$$

where η is a control parameter.

The winning global miner finally writes the updated TE-LSTM model $\mathcal{W}_i$, aggregated time cost $\mathbf{ta}_i$, predicted time cost for the next time slot $\hat{\mathbf{y}}_{i+1}$ obtained through the new model $\mathcal{W}_i$ and input $\mathbf{X}_i$, and $\Delta J(\mathcal{W}_{i-1})$ into the new global block as shown in Fig. 4.4.

A Sybil Attack Resilient Algorithm. Next, we build another LSTM network for quantity estimation of traffic reports for each road segment, called QE-LSTM. Similar to the passing time cost, the quantity of traffic reports for each road segment is also correlated to one another in a spatiotemporal manner. Therefore, we follow the same way as we design TE-LSTM to build QE-LSTM. Particularly, the ith data sample is $\mathbf{X}'_i = \{\mathbf{qa}_{i-\tau}, \ldots, \mathbf{qa}_{i-1}\}$, where $\mathbf{qa}_i = [qa_i^1, \ldots, qa_i^N]$ is the vector of the aggregated quantities of traffic reports on all the road segments in the time slot i and stored in the ith global block. Similar to Eq. (8) (note that in this case qa_i^{j*} denotes the aggregated number of reports while $y_i^{j'}$ is the predicted number of reports by QE-LSTM), (11), and (12) for TE-LSTM, in the time slot i, with the sample $\mathbf{X}'_i$ and its label $\mathbf{y}'_i = \mathbf{qa}_i$, the winning global miner can calculate the gradients $\nabla J'(\mathcal{W}'_{i-1})$, update the QE-LSTM model parameter set $\mathcal{W}'_i$, and predict the quantity of traffic

---

Algorithm 3 Defending Against Byzantine and Sybil Attacks

Input: At the ith time slot, obtained data sample $\mathbf{X}_i$, $\mathbf{X}'_i$, weights $\mathcal{W}_{i-1}$, $\mathcal{W}'_{i-1}$ from the global chain, threshold ϵ and l.

1: Winning Miner on Local Chain $j, j \in [1, N]$:
2:    ta_i^j aggregate reports $\mathcal{R}_i^j$ on road segment j.
3:    qa_i^j length of $\mathbf{t}_i^j$.
4:    $NewLocalBlock$ $ta_i^j, qa_i^j, \mathcal{R}_i^j$.
5: Winning Miner on Global Chain:
6:    **for** each road j **do**
7:      $\mathbf{ta}_i^j, \mathbf{qa}_i^j$ obtained from local chain j.
8:      **if** $|\mathbf{qa}_i^j - \hat{\mathbf{y}}'^j_{i-1}|/|\hat{\mathbf{y}}'^j_{i-1}| \leq \epsilon$ **then**
9:        $\mathbf{y}_i^j$ $\mathbf{ta}_i^j$.
10:       $\mathbf{y}'^j_i$ $\mathbf{qa}_i^j$.
11:      **else**
12:        $\mathbf{y}_i^j$ $\hat{\mathbf{y}}^j_{i-1}$.
13:        $\mathbf{y}'^j_i$ $\hat{\mathbf{y}}'^j_{i-1}$.
14:      **end if**
15:    **end for**
16:    $\nabla J(\mathcal{W}_{i-1}), \mathcal{W}_i \leftarrow$ update the TE-LSTM with $\mathbf{X}_i, \mathbf{y}_i, \mathcal{W}_{i-1}$.
17:    $\nabla J'(\mathcal{W}'_{i-1}), \mathcal{W}'_i$ update the QE-LSTM with $\mathbf{X}'_i, \mathbf{y}'_i, \mathcal{W}'_{i-1}$.
18:    $NewGlobalBlock \leftarrow \mathbf{ta}_i, \hat{\mathbf{y}}_{i+1}, \mathbf{qa}_i, \hat{\mathbf{y}}'_{i+1}, \mathcal{W}_i, \mathcal{W}'_i$.

Output: New blocks on local and global chains.

---

reports in the next time slot $\hat{\mathbf{y}}'_i$. Moreover, the winning global miner compares the predicted quantity of reports $\hat{\mathbf{y}}'_i$ from the last time slot with the finally aggregated quantity of reports $\mathbf{qa}_i$. If $|qa_i^j - \hat{y}'^j_i|/|\hat{y}'^j_i| \leq \epsilon$, the global winning miner decides that there are no Sybil attacks on this road segment, and proceeds as mentioned before. Otherwise, the global winning miner takes the predicted quantity of traffic reports $\hat{y}'^j_i$ as the real quantity, the predicted passing time cost $\hat{y}^j_i$ as the real passing time cost. It then writes the updated QE-LSTM model $\mathcal{W}'_i$, aggregated traffic report quantity $\mathbf{qa}_i$, predicted report quantity for the next time slot $\hat{\mathbf{y}}'_i$ obtained through the new model $\mathcal{W}'_i$ and input $\mathbf{X}'_i$, and $\Delta J(\mathcal{W}'_{i-1})$ into the new local block and broadcasts this new block to all the global miners.

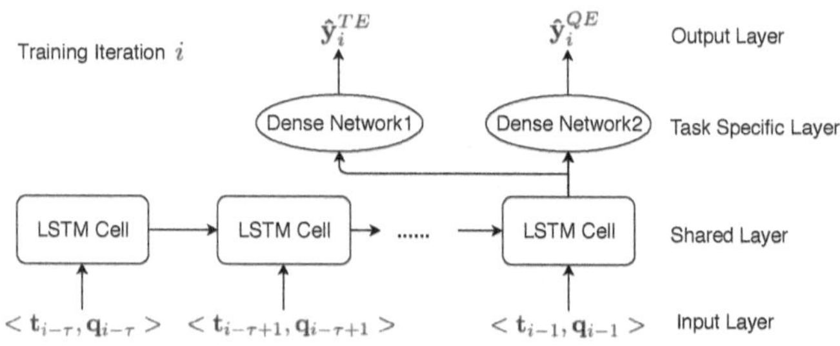

Figure 4.6. The structure of the MT-LSTM network.

The whole process for defending against Byzantine attacks and Sybil attacks and update the local and global chains is described in Algorithm 2.

Multi-task Learning based Secure Report Aggregation. Since the passing time costs and the number of vehicles on all the road segments are highly correlated as we mentioned above, we further extend our traffic report algorithm by utilizing Multi-Task Learning (MTL), which can potentially enhance the estimation of both passing time costs and vehicle quantities. In particular, the structure of our Multi-task LSTM network (MT-LSTM) is shown in Fig. 4.6. In the time slot i, the input sample for training and updating the network is $\mathbf{X}_1 = \{\mathbf{x}_{i-\tau}, \ldots, \mathbf{x}_{i-1}\}$, where $\mathbf{x}_i =< \mathbf{t}_i, \mathbf{q}_i >$, and $< \cdot, \cdot >$ is to concatenate the two vectors. The labels for input $\mathbf{X}_i$ are the target values for two specific tasks, i.e., $\mathbf{y}_i^{TE} = \mathbf{t}_i$ for time cost estimation and $\mathbf{y}_i^{QE} = \mathbf{q}_i$ for quantity estimation as defined before. The predictions of the network are $\hat{\mathbf{y}}_i^{TE}$ and $\hat{\mathbf{y}}_i^{QE}$ for the two tasks, respectively. The two tasks are trained simultaneously, where the shared LSTM layer captures the correlation among the two tasks and the task-specific layer includes an individual fully connected layer for each task. In so doing, the MT-LSTM fulfills three advantages. First, MT-LSTM helps prevent overfitting since common representations are learned[54]. Second, MT-LSTM further improves the accuracy of predicting passing time costs and report quantities by learning more information from mining the correlations among them. Third, MTL structure helps simplify the network and makes it light-weighted.

4.2.4 An Incentive Mechanism

In order to motivate users to participate in the system and submit traffic status reports, we also propose an incentive mechanism. In particular, we reward users whose reports are deemed valid when aggregated by the winning local miners. In other words, reports $t_i^j(k)$ in Eq. (4.9) are considered valid, which contribute to the final aggregated t_{ai}^j. The reporter can get rewards from TrafficChain operator, e.g., the city or Department of Transportation. In addition, since each report in TrafficChain has an ECDSA based signature, TrafficChain can easily check the authenticity of the reports.

4.2.5 Security Analysis

We first discuss the system resilience to Byzantine attacks. Under Byzantine attacks, attackers submit bogus reports containing misleading passing time on road segments. Recall the naive aggregation method in Eq. (2). A few bogus reports would severely deviate the estimated passing time cost $\bar{t}_i^j$ from its true value. In the following theorem, we prove that the impact of Byzantine attacks is limited in our Mean-Around-Krum aggregation method. We drop the subscripts and superscripts to simplify the notations.

Theorem 4. *Consider the reports for a road segment where $2f < m \leq h$. f and h denote the number of bogus reports, and that of honest reports, respectively. Let $\mathbf{t}^{(b)} = \{t_1^{(b)}, \ldots, t_f^{(b)}\}$ be all the Byzantine reports, where $t_l^{(b)} \leq t_{l+1}^{(b)}, l \in [1, f-1]$,*

$\mathbf{t}^{(h)} = \{t_1^{(h)}, \ldots, t_h^{(h)}\}$ *be all the honest reports, where* $t_l^{(h)} \le t_{l+1}^{(h)}, l \in [1, h-1]$, *and* $\{t_{min}, t_{max}\} = \{t_1^{(h)}, t_h^{(h)}\}$. *The output of Mean-Around-Krum* t^* *in the worst case is bounded by*

$$t_{min} - \frac{f}{m}(t_{max} - t_{min}) < t^* < t_{max} + \frac{f}{m}(t_{max} - t_{min}).$$

PROOF. To analyze the bounds of the output of Mean-Around-Krum t_i^{j*} in the worst case, we consider the scenario where all the Byzantine reports are included in the aggregation. So, Eq. (4.9) can be rewritten into

$$t^* = \frac{1}{m}(\sum_{i=1}^{f} t_i^{(b)} + \sum_{j=1}^{m-f} t_j^{(h)}).$$

Besides, the ground truth is $\frac{1}{h}\sum_{j=1}^{h} t_j^{(h)} \in [t_{min}, t_{max}]$, while the second term in t^* is $\sum_{j=1}^{m-f} t_j^{(h)} \in [(m-f)t_{min}, (m-f)t_{max}]$. Since we have $m > 2f$, although all bogus reports are included in the aggregation, $t(k^*)$ is still located in $[t_{min}, t_{max}]$ according to Eq. (4.10). The proof of this is given in Lemma 2 in the following.

The objective of attackers is to steer the aggregated value t_i^{j*} as small or large as possible. Therefore, we discuss the attack in two worst cases.

Case I: All the bogus reports aim to steer the passing time smaller, where $t_f^{(b)} < t_{min} \le t(k^*)$. From Eq. (4.10), we get

$$|t_1^{(b)} - t(k^*)| + \cdots + |t_f^{(b)} - t(k^*)| + |t_1^{(h)} - t(k^*)| + \ldots$$
$$+ |t_{m-f}^{(h)} - t(k^*)| <$$
$$|t_{m-f+1}^{(h)} - t(k^*)| + \cdots + |t_m^{(h)} - t(k^*)| + |t_1^{(h)} - t(k^*)| + \ldots$$
$$+ |t_{m-f}^{(h)} - t(k^*)|.$$

Due to $t_f^{(b)} < t(k^*) < t_{m-f+1}^{(h)}$, the above inequality can be rewritten into

$$ft(k^*) - \sum_{l=1}^{f} t_l^{(b)} < \sum_{l=m-f+1}^{m} t_l^{(h)} - ft(k^*)$$

$$\Rightarrow \sum_{l=1}^{f} t_l^{(b)} > 2ft(k^*) - \sum_{l=m-f+1}^{m} t_l^{(h)} > 2ft_{min} - ft_{max}$$

$$\Rightarrow \sum_{l=1}^{f} t_l^{(b)} + \sum_{l=1}^{m-f} t_l^{(h)} > 2ft_{min} - ft_{max} + (m-f)t_{min}$$

$$= (m+f)t_{min} - ft_{max}$$

$$\Rightarrow t^* > t_{min} - \frac{f}{m}(t_{max} - t_{min}) \tag{4.13}$$

Case II: All the bogus reports aim to steer the passing time greater, where $t_1^{(b)} > t_{max} \geq t(k^*)$. Similarly, we get

$$|t_1^{(b)} - t(k^*)| + \cdots + |t_f^{(b)} - t(k^*)| +$$

$$|t_{h-m+f+1}^{(h)} - t(k^*)| + \cdots + |t_h^{(h)} - t(k^*)| <$$

$$|t_{h-m+1}^{(h)} - t(k^*)| + \cdots + |t_{h-m+f}^{(h)} - t(k^*)| +$$

$$|t_{h-m+f+1}^{(h)} - t(k^*)| + \cdots + |t_h^{(h)} - t(k^*)|.$$

Because of $t_1^{(b)} > t(k^*) > t_{h-m+f}^{(h)}$, we have

$$\sum_{l=1}^{f} t_l^{(b)} - ft(k^*) < ft(k^*) - \sum_{l=h-m+1}^{h-m+f} t_l^{(h)}$$

$$\Rightarrow \sum_{l=1}^{f} t_l^{(b)} < 2ft(k^*) - \sum_{l=h-m+1}^{h-m+f} t_l^{(h)} < 2ft_{max} - ft_{min}$$

$$\Rightarrow \sum_{l=1}^{f} t_l^{(b)} + \sum_{l=1}^{m-f} t_l^{(h)} < 2ft_{max} - ft_{min} + (m-f)t_{max}$$

$$= (m+f)t_{max} - ft_{min}$$

$$\Rightarrow t^* < t_{max} + \frac{f}{m}(t_{max} - t_{min}) \tag{4.14}$$

Thus, Theorem 4 follows. $\qquad\qquad\square$

Lemma 2. *Under the same conditions as in Theorem 1, in the worst case that all Byzantine reports are included in the aggreggation, we have $t(k^*) \in [t_{min}, t_{max}]$.*

PROOF. Note that $t_{min} = t_1^{(h)}$ and $t_{max} = t_h^{(h)}$. We first consider the worst case that the Byzantine attackers aim to maliciously make $t(k^*)$ very small, where $t_f^{(b)} < t_{min}$. Thus, the report set of "$p \to I$" in Eq. (4.10) can be written as $\mathbf{t} = \{t(1), t(2), \ldots, t(m)\} = \{t_1^{(b)}, \ldots, t_f^{(b)}, t_1^{(h)}, \ldots, t_{(m-f)}^{(h)}\}$.

Define $KR(I) = \sum_{p \to I} |t(p) - t(I)|$ and $\Delta_{ij} = |t(i) - t(j)|$. Then, we have

$$KR(s) = \Delta_{1s} + \cdots + \Delta_{(s-1)s} +$$
$$\Delta_{(s+1)s} + \cdots + \Delta_{ms},$$
$$KR(s+1) = \Delta_{1(s+1)} + \cdots + \Delta_{s(s+1)} +$$
$$\Delta_{(s+2)(s+1)} + \cdots + \Delta_{m(s+1)}.$$

Note that $\Delta_{i(s+1)} = \Delta_{is} + \Delta_{s(s+1)}$ for $1 \leq i < s$ and $\Delta_{i(s+1)} = \Delta_{is} - \Delta_{s(s+1)}$ for $s + 1 < i \leq m$. Thus, we can obtain

$$KR(s+1) = \Delta_{1s} + \Delta_{2s} + \cdots + \Delta_{(s-1)s} +$$
$$(s-1)\Delta_{s(s+1)} + \Delta_{s(s+1)} + \Delta_{(s+2)s}$$
$$+ \cdots + \Delta_{ms} - (m-s-1)\Delta_{s(s+1)}$$
$$= KR(s) + (2s - m)\Delta_{s(s+1)}.$$

Due to $m \geq 2f$, we have $KR(s+1) < KR(s)$ for $1 \leq s \leq f$, which means $KR(f+1) < KR(f)$. Consequently, we get $t(k^*) \geq t_{min}$.

Similarly, in the worst case that Byzantine attackers aim to maliciously make $t(k^*)$ very large, where $t_1^{(b)} > t_{max}$, we can prove that $t(k^*) \leq t_{max}$.

Therefore, Lemma 2 follows. $\qquad\square$

Note that the attackers need to know $\mathbf{t}^{(h)}$ in order to impose the worst impact on the aggregation results, which can be challenging for attackers. Otherwise, the malicious reports $\mathbf{t}^{(b)}$ can be either too far away from or too close to $\mathbf{t}^{(h)}$. In the first case, the malicious reports may be ignored in the aggregation process due to the proposed Mean-Around-Krum scheme, while in the second case, the effect of attacks is mitigated to a large extent.

Next, we analyze Sybil attacks. Since every user submits its traffic reports with different addresses so as to mask its real identity and driving routes, Sybil attackers can take advantage of it to submit many bogus reports for each segment. To defend against Sybil attacks, our proposed QE-LSTM network detects attacks by comparing the collected number of traffic reports with the predicted one. Thus, if Sybil attacks are detected for a road segment, we discard all the reports and take the reference passing time, i.e., the predicted passing time by TE-LSTM network, as the aggregated passing time for this road segment. In so doing, the system performance is bounded by the prediction error of TE-LSTM.

Note that both accidents and attacks can result in longer than expected or predicted passing time on road segments. In fact, there are key differences between these two scenarios. Particularly, in the case of accidents, all honest users, and hence most users, will report longer than predicted passing time. However, in the case of attacks, only a few reports by attackers will include longer than expected passing time since extensive Sybil attacks will be detected. Thus, when accidents happen, the proposed TE-LSTM can correctly aggregate traffic reports and adapt to system status changes.

5 Performance Evaluation - BEMA

In this chapter, we evaluate our proposed BEMA system with real-world data. In particular, two baseline models are presented for comparison, which is regular centralized learning (single party) and distributed Heterogeneous Model Reused (HMR) method[69], respectively. With different experiment setup, we show that our decentralized system reaches competitive performance compared with the baseline models. Furthermore, we simulate attacks on calibration process and show the performance resilience. Finally, we give more analysis of simulation results and the attack resilience of the proposed system.

5.1 Data Processing

We conduct the simulation on MNIST, which is a popular machine learning dataset[32]. MNIST is an image dataset of handwritten digits, which has 60,000 training and 10,000 testing samples. Each image has a fixed-size of 28×28 pixels. To simulate the multiparty setting, we separate the dataset into different parties with different data distribution, according to Fig. 5.1. We extend a similar setting in[69], where four cases are formulated. These cases vary from 2 to 10 parties. Some of the cases are

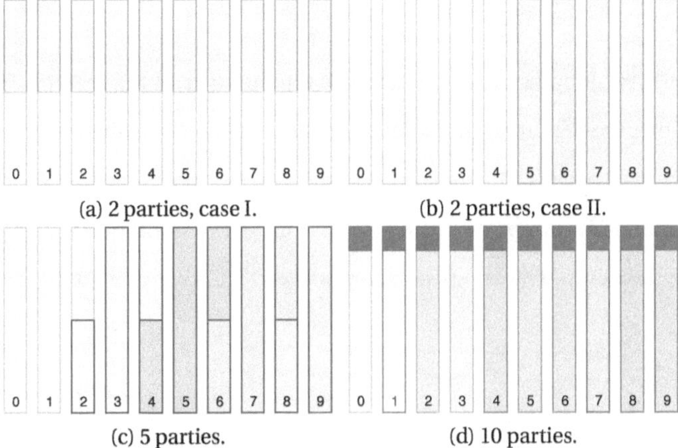

(a) 2 parties, case I.   (b) 2 parties, case II.

(c) 5 parties.   (d) 10 parties.

Figure 5.1. Data distribution in different simulation cases. Each color represents the local data on a party. There is no data overlap between different parties. In Fig. 5.1d, the red color denotes the shared public data that every party can access.

data unified distributed; some are skewed distributed, in which some parties may never see the data from some specific classes.

5.2 Baseline Models

5.2.1 Centralized Model (Single Party)

We use a regular centralized model for the benchmark of simulation. In particular, the model is equipped with a classical CNN architecture, LeNet-5. The architecture of it is two sets of convolutional layers and average pooling layers, followed by a flattening convolutional layer, then two fully-connected layers, and finally, a softmax classifier[32]. The model is trained with the whole training dataset of MNIST.

5.2.2 HMR (Distributed Multiparty Learning)

We also adopt a popular distributed multiparty learning method, HMR, as a baseline model[69]. In HMR, a center trusted server collects the local data and models from all parties. The server checks models over the union of all the data to find the calibration samples by using MPMC-margin, in Definition 2, and generates final system output by using the max-model predictor, which is introduced in Definition 1.

5.3 System Performance and Discussion

5.3.1 Simulation Setup

In our decentralized system, each party holds a LeNet-5, which has the same structure as the model in the centralized baseline model. Besides, we apply the heterogeneous model setting in the case of Fig. 5.1d, where both convolutional networks (CNN) and a fully connected neural network (ANN) are adopted. Specifically, party 1, 2, and 3 hold model of LaNet-5; party 4, 5, and 6 hold model of LaNet-4[32]; each of the rest parties holds a regular ANN, which consists of a two-hidden-layer fully connected neural nets. The setup of the calibration process is as follows. Given a calibration sample (x, y, y^-), the miner updates the corresponding local models based on Eq. (3.13) and Eq. (3.14) for *enhance* and *impair*, respectively. To make a comparison with the centralized baseline model, we define one iteration as a calibration period that 200 calibration samples are used for model calibration. This can also be called as a calibration budget of 200, which follows the same setting with the work in [69]. We apply the proposed secure MPMC-margin to find valid calibration samples and the Krum based model predictor for the final system output. Besides, δ in Eq. (3.11) and σ in Eq. (3.12) are set as 0.6 and 0.2, respectively.

5.3.2 Prediction Accuracy

We show the system prediction accuracy with the cases listed in Fig. 5.1. The comparison with the baseline models is given in each case. The results are shown in Fig. 5.2. In all the simulated cases, it can be found that after sufficient iterations, the performance of our decentralized multiparty learning method entangles with the baseline distributed multiparty learning, HMR model. Although the centralized baseline model remains the highest performance, our decentralized multiparty learning method still reaches competitive accuracy compared with the existing distributed multiparty learning. In the cases of 5-party and 10-party, the convergence speed of HMR is higher than the proposed method. However, as the proposed method focus on the decentralized system, and we applied the secure MPMC-margin to ensure the security of model calibration, it is reasonable to see the convergence speed of the proposed method is limited. In spite of this, we are still confident to conclude that the proposed decentralized multiparty learning is a decent alternative model to the existing distributed one.

5.3.3 Attack Resilience

In this part, we further test the system to attack resilience with the designed attacks. As we mentioned in Section 3.1.2, there are two types of critical attacks in the system. Type I attack is the broadcast of malicious local models, and type II is the broadcast of bogus calibration messages. In type I attack, the malicious party

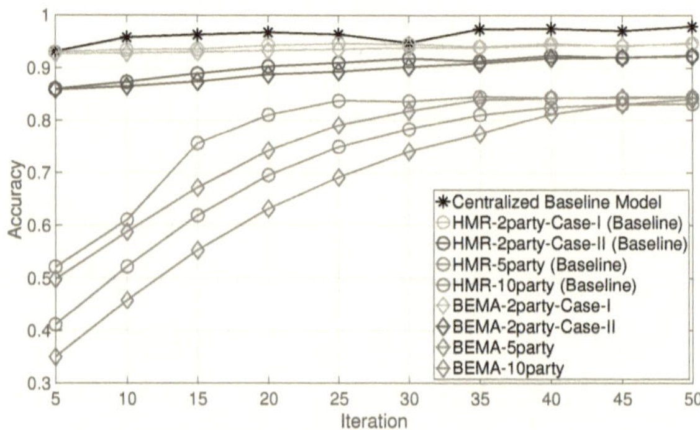

Figure 5.2. System prediction accuracy. The comparison results between BEMA and the baseline models.

broadcasts the arbitrary model information, e.g., the attacker professes the model is trained with a class of y, while which is actually trained on the class of y'. There are two mechanisms designed in the proposed system to defend such an attack. The first is to set up restrictions when a new participant wants to add his local model in the system. From Eq. (3.2), the newly added models have to be performing fairly close to the existing OP's models and obtain the approval from the OP before they can join the system legally. Thus, the restriction helps prevent malicious local models to be joined into the system. Second, all the model calibration processes are public and can be verified by every participant. Thus, as long as the calibration messages are valid, the models on the blockchain cannot be tampered arbitrarily and will be updated in the right direction. To validate the calibration messages, the secure MPMC-margin and Krum based Model Predictor are proposed. In the simulation, we launch type II attack, where bogus calibration messages are generated and test the attack resilience of the proposed method.

In particular, three cases are simulated. In the first case, we continue to use the setup in Fig. 5.1d, where there are a total of 10 parties in the system. A certain percentage of bogus calibration messages are broadcasted in the system, where the bogus messages are generated by Eq. (3.1). In other words, for any calibration sample (x, y, y^-) that makes $\rho(x, y, y^-) > 0$, the attacker can maliciously broadcast calibration sample as (x, y^-, y), which makes $\rho(x, y^-, y) < 0$. Thus the bogus message is generated. If any model is calibrated by such a sample, it is maliciously tampered. In the second case, we further divide each party in the first case into two parties. The local dataset of each party is also averagely separated into two parties. Similar to the third case, we divide each party in the first case into five. The results of system prediction accuracy under the above three cases are shown in Table 5.1. For each case, we make a comparison with HMR method, where the simulation setting is the same. All the results are the system prediction accuracy after 50 iterations of model calibration. From the table, it can be found the proposed method outperforms HMR under type II attack. Under 10% and 20% of bogus messages, BEMA still outputs competitive performance. Under 50% of bogus messages, the performance of HMR decays obviously, while the influence on the proposed method is limited. The reason for the results mainly comes from two aspects. First, regarding the calibration samples validation, we have constraints in Eq. (3.11) and (3.12) to help verify the validity of broadcasted calibration message. Thus some of the bogus calibration messages are completely ignored by the miner in the system, while HMR applies all of them. Besides, as we analyzed in Theorem 3, the influence of the attacks in each calibration iteration is bounded by applying the

Table 5.1. System prediction accuracy under attacks. In HMR, MPMC-margin and Max-Model Predictor are used for model calibration and generating system output. In BEMA, the proposed secure MPMC-margin and Krum based Model Predictor are used.

Percentage of Bogus Messages	0%	10%	20%	50%
HMR (10-Party)	0.8320	0.7926	0.7397	0.5849
BEMA (10-Party)	**0.8401**	**0.8372**	**0.8134**	**0.7692**
HMR (20-Party)	**0.8178**	0.7631	0.6959	0.5281
BEMA (20-Party)	0.8023	**0.7895**	**0.7710**	**0.7395**
HMR (50-Party)	**0.7587**	0.6945	0.6120	0.4162
BEMA (50-Party)	0.7316	**0.7228**	**0.7012**	**0.6804**

secure MPMC-margin. Second, regarding the system predictor, HMR uses the max-model predictor, which only selects a single model to output the prediction score on a certain data sample. It is obvious that the prediction score is easily corrupted once a malicious model is selected. By applying the proposed Krum based model predictor, our BEMA aggregates the output of multiple local models to generate the prediction on a certain data sample. Thus, the attack on the system prediction accuracy is further mitigated.

5.4 Discussion

In the simulation above, we first show that BEMA can reach competitive performance compared with HMR, an existing distributed multiparty learning method. Then we simulate the attacks to show the attack resilience of the proposed method. Besides, we also find the setup of system parameters, i.e., δ, and σ, influences the efficiency of the system prediction accuracy and attack resilience. δ and σ in Eq. (3.11) and (3.12) are used for verifying the calibration sample. A lower δ or a higher σ reflects that the calibration sample becomes more easily to pass the verification.

As more samples pass the verification in each iteration, the convergence speed of system prediction accuracy gets higher. However, if the attacks are launched in the samples, the system is more likely to be misled as the samples are easy to be trusted. Conversely, a higher δ or a lower σ reflects a lower convergence speed, yet a higher attack resilience level. All in all, we conclude that BEMA is a decentralized multiparty learning system that is reliable on both the system performance and the attack resilience.

6 Performance Evaluation - TrafficChain

In this chapter, we conduct simulations to evaluate the performance of our TrafficChain system and focus on its information accuracy and attack resistance. In particular, we first show the performance of TE-LSTM network on predicting traffic statuses and compare with other machine learning methods. Then, we launch Byzantine attacks and Sybil attacks in the system, and test the resilience of TrafficChain to them respectively. Meanwhile, we compare with other existing byzantine resilient aggregation methods. At last, we further analyze and discuss the simulation results.

6.1 Dataset

The dataset we use for simulations is a public dataset of Chicago city[45]. Specifically, we use the dataset of Chicago Traffic Tracker-Congestion Estimates by Traffic Segments (CEbTS). The city of Chicago divides the streets into segments, where each segment is typically a half-mile long in one direction of traffic. CEbTS gives the estimated speed for 1250 road segments covering 300 miles of streets, which is obtained by continuously monitoring and analyzing GPS traces of Chicago Transit Authority (CTA) buses. Speed data is generated every 10 minutes for the period of

Attributes	Description	Type
Time	Date and time	D&T
Segment ID	Unique arbitrary number to represent each segment.	#
Street	Street name of the traffic segment.	T
Direction	Traffic flow direction for the segment.	T
Speed	Estimated speed in miles per hour.	#
Start&End Latitudes	Latitudes of the start and end of the segment.	#
Start&End Longitudes	Longitudes of the start and end of the segment.	#
Bus Count	Number of buses passed in the time slot.	#

Table 6.1. Main attributes of data in CEbTS.

the year 2018, leading to a total of 50,457,500 data samples for 1250 road segments over 40,366 time slots. The main attributes of data in CEbTS are shown in Table 6.1. '#, T, D&T' represents number, text, and date & time data types, respectively. It should be noticed that a GPS trace is required for estimating speed on a road segment. Therefore, the speed information is missing in the dataset when there is no bus on a road segment, e.g., in some time slots of off-peak hours. In this case, the speed is marked as '-1' to reflect data unavailability. Besides, the speed '0' reflects full or partial street closure due to an unexpected event. For the longitudes and latitudes of start and end points of the segment, the ending latitude and longitude for a segment will be the same as the starting latitude and longitude for the segment next to it.

6.2 Data Pre-Processing

As shown in Fig. 6.1, we select the rectangular area in the City of Chicago as our area of interest, which contains 419 road segments. The CEbTS dataset provides estimated traffic speeds on the road segments, while our TrafficChain system collects the time cost for each road segment. Since each road segment is set to half a mile long, we calculate the time cost in seconds for road segment i as $t_i = \frac{0.5}{v_i} \times 3600$, where v_i is the estimated speed (mph) on the road segment i. Moreover, we set an upper limit of 600 seconds to the time cost for a road segment, which refers to street closure.

As mentioned before, the CEbTS dataset has missing data marked as '-1'. We fill the missing data with the most recent estimated traffic speed. This is because most missing data happen during off-peak hours when the traffic speed usually remains stable. Besides, recall that there are 40,366 time slots in total. We only use the data in the first select 10,000 (24.77%) time slots as training samples, and use the data in the rest time slots as testing samples.

6.3 Performance of TE-LSTM

6.3.1 Network setup

We first evaluate the performance of TE-LSTM in traffic reports aggregation. We implement it in a multi-task architecture, with the prediction for time cost on each road segment being a task. The hard parameter sharing structure is adopted[54]. The lookback window size is set to 24, which is to analyze 4 hours' history data for making prediction in the next time slot of ten minutes. So, the size of each training

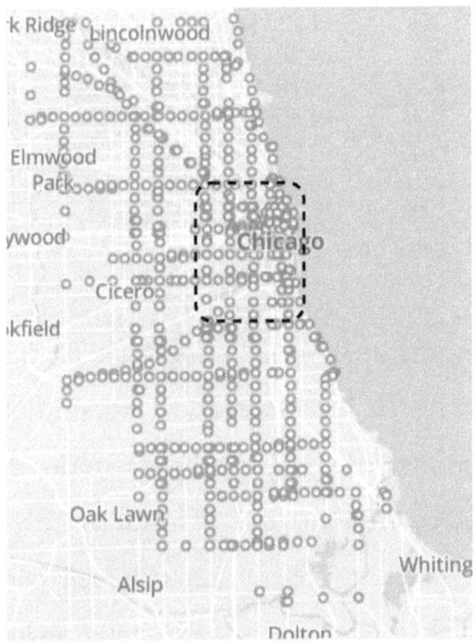

Figure 6.1. The data in CEbTS. Each point is a road segment, and there are 1250 points in total. The dashed line rectangle shows our area of interest, which contains a total of 419 road segments.

sample has a dimension of 24×419, and the label is 1×419. We set the output of the parameter sharing layer to 128 nodes. Each task-specific layer maps the previous output to the particular road time cost with size $128 \rightarrow 1$. Normalization is also performed for the added at the input of the network. We choose Mean Square Error (MSE) as the loss function.

6.3.2 Simulation Results

Table 6.2 presents the Root of Mean Square Error (RMSE) of TE-LSTM and other popular time series data prediction methods, including RNN, ARIMA, logistic regression, and linear regression. Since our TE-LSTM network is implemented as a

ID	TE-LSTM	RNN	ARIMA	Logistic	Linear
#1	19.80	22.45	20.20	23.79	29.57
#25	18.79	19.92	19.24	23.62	28.44
#50	19.47	21.81	21.24	24.75	30.25
#100	13.82	16.23	13.97	21.70	27.44
Overall	18.58	19.93	19.92	23.57	29.14

Table 6.2. RMSE of TE-LSTM, RNN, ARIMA, logistic regression, and linear regression.

multi-task structure, we show the testing results for some particular road segments, i.e., segments 1, 25, 50, 100, as well as the overall results for all the road segments. We can see that our TE-LSTM network outperforms all the other methods both in individual prediction for each road segment and in overall prediction.

Note that LSTM is usually difficult to be well trained when the dimension of the training samples gets huge. However, as the multi-task structure is employed, the parameter sharing layer can be pre-trained and only the task-specific layer parameters need to be updated, whose size is relatively small. We show the training speed on task-specific layers with the pre-trained parameter sharing layer in Fig. 6.2. We can observe that TE-LSTM can converge fast.

6.4 Attack Resilience

Next, we test the performance of TrafficChain in terms of resilience to Byzantine and Sybil attacks.

6.4.1 Resilience to Byzantine Attacks

We launch Byzantine attacks in the system by adding Gaussian noises to the traffic reports. Particularly, we select three of the busiest road segments for simulations,

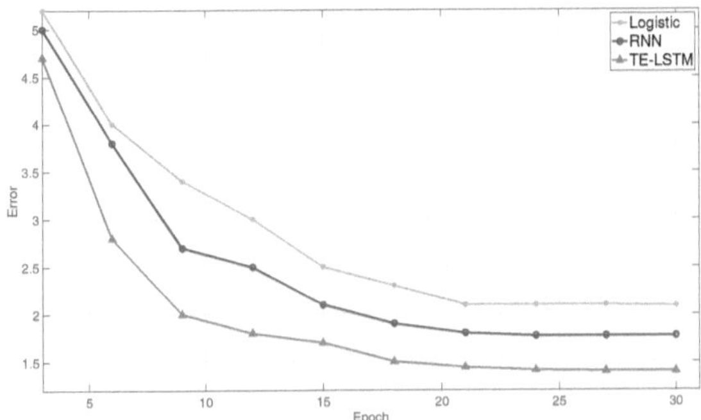

Figure 6.2. Average training loss of TE-LSTM, RNN, and logistic regression. It shows the training speed of our task-specific LSTM, and comparing models, i.e., RNN and Logistic Regression. The horizontal axis is the training epochs, and the vertical one is normalized MSE error with the unit of $10^{(-3)}$.

i.e., 889, 922, and 1295, respectively. We set the number of the reports equal to the number of buses on a road segment. A certain ratio of reports are added with Gaussian noises $|\mathcal{N}(0, \sigma^{(M)})|$. To simulate a practical scenario, we also add Gaussian noises $\mathcal{N}(0, \sigma^{(H)})$ to honest reports too. For each of the three road segments, we use the data on a particular day to test our MT-LSTM aggregation method. We compare our proposed MT-LSTM aggregation with two state-of-the-art schemes, i.e., l-nearest[11] and marginal median (MarMed)[70], as well as with using TE-LSTM only without the proposed Mean-Around-Krum scheme.

In particular, for road segment #889, we divide the time slots in a day into four parts as shown in Fig. 6.3. In the first 40% of time slots, no attack is launched, which means all the reports are submitted honestly. In the first 40% to 60% time slots, we add malicious Gaussian noises to 30% of the reports. In the first 60% to 80% time slots, we add malicious Gaussian noises to 50% of the reports. In the rest time

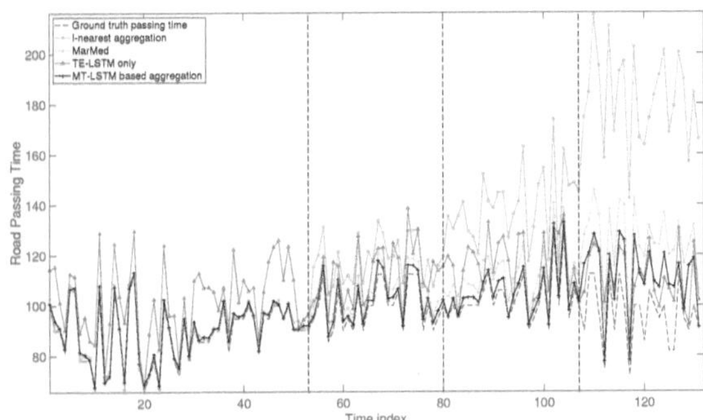

Figure 6.5. Resilience to Byzantine attacks on road segment #1295. $\sigma^{(M)} = 120$. Different from the setup in Fig. 6.3 and Fig. 6.4, in four parts of data separated by dashed lines, 0%, 20%, 40%, and 60% of the reports are attacked, respectively.

slots, 80% of the reports are attacked. The results are shown in Fig. 6.3. In the first 40% time lots, all four schemes can obtain aggregated time cost fairly close to the ground truth. Among them, TE-LSTM returns the worst performance caused by prediction errors, which indicates the effectiveness of Mean-Around-Krum. When it comes to the second part, since 30% of the reports are attacked, the regular l-nearest method has the worst performance among all the schemes because it selects l-nearest reports to the mean of all reports to aggregate, which gets higher due to the attacks. Our MT-LSTM aggregation slightly outperforms MarMed. Then, when 50% of the reports are attacked, both MarMed and regular l-nearest method include a number of attacked reports for aggregation and hence achieve degraded results, while our MT-LSTM aggregation scheme still obtains aggregated time cost close to the ground truth. In the last data part where 80% reports are attacked, our MT-LSTM aggregation inevitably includes some attacked reports for aggregation, but its performance is still better than the other two aggregation methods. The simulation results on the other two road segments are shown in Fig. 6.4 and Fig. 6.5, where $\sigma^{(M)}$ is set to 100 and 120, respectively. We can observe that the proposed MT-LSTM based aggregation can always achieve the best results close to the ground truth.

6.4.2 Resilience to Sybil Attacks

Recall that Sybil attackers create many fake identities to submit malicious traffic reports. Our QE-LSTM detects Sybil attacks by comparing the number of collected traffic reports with the predicted one. Similar to TE-LSTM, we add a task-specific layer for predicting the number of reports for each road segment. The RMSE of the QE-LSTM is used to estimate whether Sybil attacks exist. In particular, let $e^{(q)}$ be the RMSE of QE-LSTM. If $|x' - \hat{x}'| \leq e^{(q)}$, where x' and $\hat{x}'$ are the total number of collected reports and the quantity prediction from QE-LSTM, respectively, there is no Sybil attack, and Mean-Around-Krum is employed to finally aggregate the time cost. Otherwise, it is determined that there are Sybil attacks. In this case, only the outputs of QE-LSTM and TE-LSTM are used for generating the final result and updating both LSTMs.

We first show the performance of QE-LSTM and MT-LSTM on the prediction of the number of traffic reports, and then evaluate their resilience to both Byzantine and Sybil attacks. Table 6.3 shows the prediction results of our QE-LSTM and MT-LSTM, compared with other prediction methods, including RNN, logistic regression, and linear regression. Particularly, bus counts information in CEbTS is used as the ground truth of the number of reports. We can see that MT-LSTM achieves

ID	MT-LSTM	QE-LSTM	RNN	Logistic	Linear
#889	2.20	2.54	3.05	3.63	4.2
#922	1.76	2.42	2.88	3.78	4.59
#1295	2.43	2.49	2.59	3.16	4.21
Overall	2.21	2.60	2.89	3.67	4.48

Table 6.3. RMSE results of MT-LSTM and QE-LSTM on predicting the quantity of passing vehicles compared with RNN, logistic and linear regression. The RMSE of three particular roads with segment IDs #889, #922, #1295, and the overall average RMSE on all roads are given. Bus counts information is used as the ground truth.

better results than QE-LSTM since it can learn more information, and that both MT-LSTM and QE-LSTM outperform the other state-of-the-art methods.

Fig. 6.6 shows the system performance under both Byzantine and Sybil attacks. The testing data includes a whole day period. In the first 20 time slots, there is no attack. After that, in each time slot, one more malicious report is added which reports the time cost of 600s. Four aggregation methods are tested, including regular l-nearest, MarMed, QE-LSTM, plus TE-LSTM, MT-LSTM. As the time index increases, there are more and more malicious reports, the regular l-nearest aggregation method is severely affected. MarMed obtains competitive performance when only a limited amount of Sybil attacks are launched. However, as there are over 20 malicious reports, i.e., when malicious reports are more than honest reports, MarMed gets very poor results. In this case, QE-LSTM and MT-LSTM will detect Sybil attacks due to $|x' - \hat{x}'| > e^{(q)}$, and solely use the prediction results of TE-LSTM as the time cost. Although the accuracy of time cost decreases under Sybil attacks, both QE-LSTM + TE-LSTM and MT-LSTM can obtain significantly better results than the other schemes.

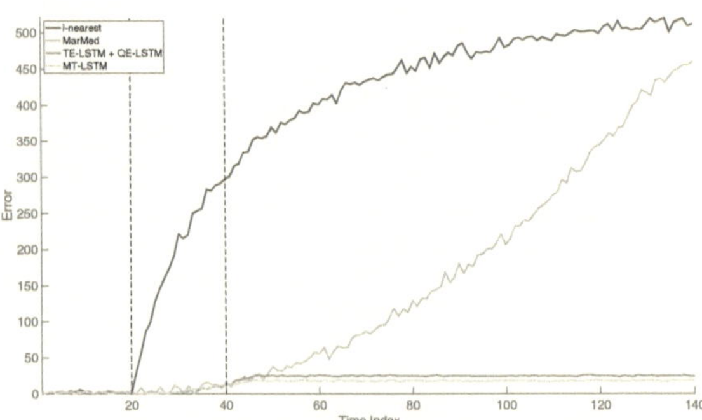

Figure 6.6. The system performance under both Byzantine and Sybil attacks. The vertical axis means the average error of all segments. From the first vertical dash line (20th time slot), the attacks are added, where each time slot is added by one more arbitrary report than the previous time slot. From the second dash line, the LSTM agent notices the attack and the information from reports are eliminated.

6.5 TrafficChain Update Efficiency

Since, in practice, there can be a huge number of vehicles in a city participating in the system, the computing load in the system can be heavy. To address this problem, we have developed a two-layer blockchain architecture to enhance system efficiency. In this section, we test the time consumption of reports collection and model update by comparing TrafficChain with a normal single blockchain. In particular, the single blockchain collects reports from all vehicles in the system, and aggregate them with the regular l-nearest method. In TrafficChain, local miners first aggregate the traffic reports for their corresponding road segments and then submit reports to global miners for the model update. Since traffic reports aggregation is conducted by local miners in a distributed fashion, the reports collection process is much faster. Since the number of local chains is much smaller than the number of all the vehicles in the system, the model update process is much faster.

6.5.1 Block Update Efficiency

Fig. 6.7 shows the results of time consumption of building a global block on TrafficChain and on a regular blockchain. The simulation is based on a Mobile Adhoc Network MANET in NetSim emulator[2] supported by a PC with 16GB of RAM and Intel i7 at 2.8Ghz. From the results, we can see that when there are fewer than 100 vehicles in the system, TrafficChains spends more time than a regular blockchain to collect reports and build a new global block. However, when there are more than 100 vehicles, the time needed by TrafficChain to build a new block remains relatively stable since the number of local chains remains the same, while the time needed by a regular blockchain to build a new block increases significantly.

6.5.2 Report Aggregation Efficiency

Since the proposed deep neural network can be pre-trained offline, the time cost for running our proposed scheme mainly comes from two parts. One part is due to the online updating of the trained deep neural network, which is to calculate the gradients in the SGD algorithm as in Eq. (4.11). The other is due to the Mean-Around-Krum algorithm. Comparing with the second part, the time cost of online updating is negligible. The time complexity of Mean-Around-Krum depends on sorting the reports. As we use quicksort as the sorting algorithm, the time complexity of Mean-Around-Krum is lower and upper bounded by $O(n)$ and $O(nlog(n))$, respectively, when sorting n reports. On a PC with 16G RAM and Intel i7 CPU, our

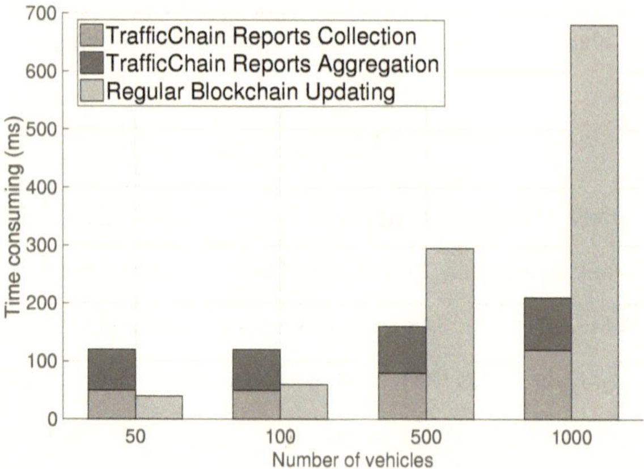

Figure 6.7. Time consumption for building a new global block. Green and blue bars are the time needed for reports collection and LSTM based aggregation processes in TrafficChain, respectively. The light blue bar is the updating process for a regular single blockchain.

aggregation method only takes 6s to aggregate the reports for 2800 road segments in each time slot.

7 Conclusions

This book focuses on an application of edge computing. In particular, we propose a blockchain-empowered secure multiparty learning system over edge devices, which is called BEMA. Different from the existing multiparty learning meth-ods, the superiority of BEMA is twofold. First, our system extends the regular dis-tributed multiparty learning into a fully decentralized structure, where each party is allowed to hold a heterogeneous model. Second, we carefully concern security issues in the decentralized system, where two types of Byzantine attacks are for-mulated. We propose "off-chain" and "on-chain" mining schemes for attack de-fending. Furthermore, theoretical analysis is given to show the performance of the proposed system and the system resilience under Byzantine attacks. Simula-tion results on the well-known machine learning data show that the efficacy and reliability of BEMA.

In this book, we furhter have developed TrafficChain, a secure and privacy-preserving decentralized traffic information collection system. In particular, we have designed a two-layer blockchain architecture for efficient communication and block updating in TrafficChain. Besides, a privacy-preserving scheme has been devised to protect users' identities and driving routes. Moreover, we have considered two critical kinds of attacks, i.e., Byzantine and Sybil attacks, in TrafficChain, and developed novel deep learning based schemes to defend against them. Simulation results show that TrafficChain is both resilient to those attacks and efficient in generating new blocks.